DEDICATION

~

To my father and mentor, Dr. Allen Mendler. I am honored to take your work to the next level. Thank you for opening doors and allowing me to burst through. I am forever grateful. I love you.

ACKNOWLEDGEMENTS

~

Elijah and Brooklyn, Thank you for the joy you provide. I am so grateful I get to be your daddy. I love you both times infinity.

Renee, Thank you for the artwork that fills our home. Your talent and passion amaze me every day. I love you.
www.reneemendlerart.com

To my mom, brother, sister, sister in law, brother in law, nieces and nephews, Family over everything, always. I love you.

Jon Crabbe, Elizabeth Sherwood, Dianne Long, Colleen Zawadzki, and our staff at the Teacher Learning Center, Your expertise, professionalism, and dedication to our business are always appreciated.

Jimmy Cases, Jeff Zoul, Todd Whitaker, Joe Sanfelippo, Kayla Delzer, LaVonna Roth, Tom Murray, Brianna Hodges, and everyone else at #WGEDD, Thanks for inviting me to be part of such an amazing group. I am honored.

Baruti Kafele, You inspire so many. Thanks for the mentorship and the forward. I appreciate you. Please follow him on twitter @Principalkafele.

Kathleen Skeals, Thank you for editing this book. I appreciate our friendship and all you do for kids. Please follow her on twitter @ Kathleenskeals.

To all my social media followers and friends, This career is not possible without the knowledge and inspiration you give me every day. I am grateful to each of you.

To everyone at Developmental Resources, Especially Phil Price and Keli Wickersham, I am thankful and humbled to be such a major part of your conference every year.

Finally, to all the members of my recovery meetings, Without you none of this is possible. "Keep coming back it works if you work it you're worth it so work it."

Special thanks to Lisa Hartel & Blue Water Printing, For cover design and printing services. www.bwprintingandmailing.com

FORWARD

~

I first met Brian Mendler a few years ago at the National School Discipline conference in Atlanta. At the time I just finished my best selling book titled, The Teacher 50. Brian asked me to attend his breakout session and offer feedback. Within minutes I knew his energy and enthusiasm for the toughest kids were contagious. Rarely does a person speak openly and candidly about personal obstacles. He told stories of reading difficulties as a child, growing up in the shadow of a brilliant older sibling, and attending addiction recovery meetings for the past 16 years. Before agreeing to write this forward I made sure all those stories were included in this book as each provides a powerful lesson for all kids. During his presentation in Atlanta he spoke of a special teacher who used seven words to help change his life. The final chapter is dedicated to him. When I asked Brian why he chose this title he said, "The number one thing learned in addiction recovery is every time I have a problem with someone or something I am a big part of the cause. If I change me I almost always change everything around me. As a kid I always blamed everyone else. If I failed a class the teacher was dumb. If I was cut from a team the coach was clueless. The truth is I was afraid to look at my own behavior first. By viewing myself as the problem I am always in control. Imagine if everyone in school looked at him or herself first in every situation. Kids love to blame teachers and vice versa. The truth is all of us need to watch our mouths because words matter." Through personal experience this book reminds us we have a moral responsibility to do whatever it takes to save the most challenging kids. It provides true, transparent resources, interventions, and prevention strategies all educators can use immediately. This book will refresh your commitment and desire to work with all kids.

My top ten takeaways are:

- Retrain your brain.
- 2nd to last word is best.
- Walking away = strength.
- Stay personally connected to kids without taking personally what they do and say.
- Apologize to kids and parents that are upset, even when doing nothing wrong.
- Five specific reasons students misbehave and exactly what to do about it.
- Always thank a student *before* they complete a request.
- The "Five W's" of defusing.
- Why I should feel "grateful" when a student "unloads" on me.
- Prevention phrases.

This book is a quick and easy read and makes a profound impact. It focuses on specific strategies educators can use immediately in their classrooms and schools. From carpet on the desk for the annoying pen tapper to a specific process for "defusing any kid anywhere at anytime," to dozens of the latest websites for using songs to teach content. This book provides something for everyone and is sure to change your perspective and attitude toward your most challenging students.

- Baruti K. Kafele

TABLE OF CONTENTS

~

PROLOGUE

~

That One Teacher

It is not easy getting kicked out of public school, but I was able to do it. I will tell you later exactly why but just about all of my problems stem from a pretty severe learning struggle I had as a kid and somewhat have as an adult. I believe reading is the number one skill kids struggle with in school making it a really hard place. Really good readers live on honor roll and win awards. Great public speakers live in trouble and detention. My major problems began in fourth grade. Until fourth grade I looked at pictures and listened to my friends. Fourth grade is the year things got really bad for me. My teacher's name was Mrs. Mills (not her real name) and I truly deep down believe she did not like kids. It is a Tuesday night and the homework assignment is one through twenty-one, odds. A classic assignment many teachers give kids. It takes me two hours to do two problems. I finish the second problem and say to my mom, "I can't do anymore of these. I am exhausted." My mom says, "Ok Brian, that is fine. No problem. Except, you will to have to live with the consequences." I reply, "Consequences? Why are there consequences? I just worked for two straight hours on this and there will be consequences? You must be kidding." My mother looks me directly in the eyes, gets up and starts washing the dishes. To this day she has yet to answer. I find out quickly what she means the next day when I get to school. Mrs. Mills does not say good morning to kids. She does not ask how we are doing. She does not ask what is going on in our lives. Instead she barks, "Get out your homework." I get out my homework and for a minute feel pretty good about what I had done the night before. Two hours to do two problems. The good feeling does not last. Somehow, Mrs. Mills has time in her day to wander around the room to every single kid, with her grade book open and pen in her ear. She gets to me and condescendingly asks, "Where are the rest of these, Brian?" My reply, "Well, last night I..." She cuts me off, "Last night I? Last night I? I am sure you have a story for where the rest of these problems are because you always have a story for everything. I think you are lazy. I think you are unmotivated. I think you need to try harder." Deep down I feel like crying. I am ten and my friends are around which means crying is not an option. Instead, I fight back with my mouth. I say, "Maybe I am lazy and maybe I am unmotivated or maybe you are a shi**y teacher. Have you ever considered that? I think you have no idea how to teach. If they let you go to teacher school anyone in the whole world can become a teacher."

Thankfully, in sixth grade at my new school I have one teacher tell me seven words that change my life. In two minutes he accomplishes more with me than any other teacher between kindergarten and sixth grade. Keep reading to learn what they are. It is now December 23, 2001 and a snowy Monday night in Buffalo NY. I pace outside the room at Kenmore Presbyterian Church, occasionally peeking in. My heart is racing. Do I belong here? Who are these people? Will they understand? I can't do it. I turn to leave and bump squarely into an older gentleman about six feet three inches tall with gray thinning hair. I glance up and our eyes briefly meet. I take a step past him and feel my left arm squeeze. "You look like an addict. Come with me." He pulls me into the room. "My name is Kevin M. We don't use last names here just first names and first letters of our last names." My left leg shakes nervously as I peer under the brim of the baseball hat pulled low over my eyes. At 7:30 the door shuts. Plaques on tables read, "Who you see here, what you hear here, when you leave here let it stay here." A man sits at the head of the oval table and looks directly at me. "We have a new member. What is your name?"

Me: "My name is Brian M."

Chris: "Welcome Brian. Why are you here?"

Me: "I am here because I have a problem with gambling."

Chris: "No, you don't."

Me: (taken aback and agitated) "Yes, I do."

Chris: "No, you don't."

Me: (now really aggravated and much louder) "Who the "F" are you? Yes. I. Do!" Kevin grabs my arm again, "Dude, chill. Let him explain."

Chris: "I am sorry. I don't mean to offend or upset you. The biggest misconception people have when entering these rooms is gambling, drinking, cocaine, overeating, are the problems. They are not. They are the solutions to your problems. There is a good chance you don't even know what your problems are. Do me a favor and close your eyes (I did). Picture the biggest pile of dirt you can imagine. Picture the biggest shovel you can lift. Every time you gamble or use drugs you take a heaping scoop of dirt and dump it directly on your problems because you don't want to face them. In these rooms we dig out problems, force you to face them, and teach you new solutions."

This moment helped so much because I always believed addiction was part of me. Everyone said, "Oh Brian? Hide your purse, he has a gambling problem." Instantly, this man separates addiction from me. Now, addiction is an option in a stratosphere of choices. If I face my problems and pick different solutions, I have a chance. Fast-forward almost seventeen years. I still attend meetings every week. By now, I learned my real problem was a deep dark feeling of inadequacy in my life. Like my best effort was never going to be good enough. Growing up in the shadow of a brilliant older sibling, I wanted to be noticed. Why tell all this? Last August I worked a stretch of 24 cities in 31 days. I watched teachers returning from summer break, getting class lists, and comparing student names. I kept hearing them use the phrase, "behavior problem" when describing a student. At first, I said nothing because doing so meant telling my whole story, and I simply was not ready. For 15.5 years I lived two completely parallel lives, both really good. I was a teacher all day and in addiction recovery meetings at night. Rarely did they intersect. Occasionally I told individual students and parents. My close family and friends have always known. This day a teacher says,

"Oh, her? That girl is a never-ending behavior problem. Oh him? He's a constant behavior problem." Finally I impulsively say (my meds clearly not yet kicked in), "Stop! You guys please stop! I'm sorry. I keep hearing the phrase 'behavior problem.' There is no such thing as a behavior problem. Behaviors for kids are not the problem. They are solutions to problems. The real problem is her desperate need for attention. Her solution is to make weird noises. If educators help students dig out problems and teach new solutions we will change lives forever.

CHAPTER 1

~

Non Negotiables for Success with the Toughest Kids

- **You Have to Like Them:** This means looking at every situation from the students' perspective first. It means asking to have them in your class. It means taking a turn with someone else's most challenging student. It means pretending when you don't feel like it. The toughest kids must believe if we never see them again we will be equally as devastated as if we never see our own child again. Sadly, many feel the opposite.

- **You Must be Willing to Change Yourself:** Succeeding with the toughest kids is not possible if you are unwilling to look at yourself first. This does not mean that you are the sole cause of the problem; far from it. This simply means that you start by looking in the mirror first every time you have a problem with anyone or anything in your life. If you fix yourself, you can fix the problem. It is almost always that easy.

- **Questions are Better than Statements:** Whenever possible rephrase statements to questions when working with the toughest kids. For oppositional kids, questions are kryptonite and statements fuel. Instead of, "We don't talk to adults like that!" Try, "Why do you think it is ok to talk to adults that way? Where in your life have you learned that language is appropriate? Do you know what you sound like when using that type of language?

1

Don't you believe you are better than that?" Then, be prepared to really listen to the student's answers.

- **Never Take it Personally:** Early in my career a colleague said to feel grateful if a kid "flips out" on me. Often in life we unload our biggest frustrations on people we care for most. True or not, it is a good way to look at things. Stay personally connected to your toughest kids without taking personally what they do and say. Focus on what is said instead of how it is said.

- **Second to Last Word is Best:** It seems many teachers are born "last word" type people. Retraining the brain to become a second to last word person with kids allows us out of almost any arguments or power struggles. "Thanks" is a great last word. "I think I saw you drop that piece of paper and I'd appreciate if you picked it up! Thanks."

- **Walking Away = Strength:** You must see avoiding a power struggle as winning. Walking away is critical. Prepare to hear the student mumble a few inappropriate things under his breath. He is really saying, "Right now I have to call you a couple names under my breath because I don't want to look like a wimp in front of the class…" Keep walking away.

- **People Over Product, Always:** Firemen and women are amazing. Grown adults waiting to run in burning buildings to save people they never met, mostly for free. The rules are simple: save anything alive first, starting with people and pets. Destroy anything in the path, including valuables, to focus on saving lives. This mindset is fundamental with the toughest kids. Sometimes we have to blow up the math lesson to focus on the individuals in front of us. Caring about the person must always come before anything you are trying to teach the person. If you can do this, the person will learn anything you want to teach them.

- **Some is Better Than None:** If I reach one kid it is worth it. Even if I do not reach ten. Measure success by baseball standards. Three out of ten is an all star. Decide some is always better than none. Decide late is better than not at all. Be willing to negotiate almost anything not involving safety.

- **Private is Better Than Public:** The audience plays a role in every performance. Move kids away from their friends when talking about anything personal. Rewards, awards, behavior charts, tickets and stickers are most effective when used privately. Praise and correct as privately as possible. Always ask before posting graded work. Tell students how much you value privacy and promise never to purposely embarrass them in front of each other. Ask them to reciprocate.

- **Change is a Roller Coaster Ride:** If a student has a solid Monday do not be surprised if he disrupts on Tuesday. For some kids it is literally good hour followed by bad hour. Be prepared for this. Do not let it surprise you. The goal is to see it as the stock market: a little more up than down. And, remember, during the down cycle, kids need you most.

- **Focus on the Journey:** Recently, my fully potty trained four-year-old son pooped his pants. In the bathroom, I was frustrated helping him change. "Eli, you are four years old. It is not ok to go in your pants. When feeling pressure on your stomach run right to the bathroom." Ever try explaining to a four-year-old what needing to poop feels like? It is not easy. A split second later, I had a strange experience almost as if I were watching the interaction between us rather than participating in it. Flashbacks of friends and family with older kids: "Embrace it. Enjoy the journey. Be present now because in a blink they are teenagers." I look at my son, a tear running down his cheek, "It's ok Buddy. We all make mistakes. It's fine. I promise." A moment later, his chin is tucked under my neck as I help him change. In this small moment, a crappy (literally) moment is turned into a special interaction never forgotten.

3

Each of us has the ability to control the attitude we take to each situation and the effort we put in. Embrace the journey and do not allow every challenging behavior ruin your day. Mental toughness is the single most important component to working with kids. It is not always easy, but embracing the journey makes the ride more enjoyable.

Concluding Thought: Somehow my wife gets "the best deal ever" on shoes every day. She thinks because the price tag, which says $69.99, has a line through it, and now says $39.99 it is a great deal! What really happens is the shoe company makes the shoes. Then says, "Hmmm. What do we charge? $39.99." Then they hire a marketing company who says, "No silly! You write the number $69.99 on the tag. Then, take a red pen and cross it out. Scribble the number $39.99 next to it. Print a big red sign that says, 'Clearance.' They will get a great deal and tell all their friends." My wife bites. Kids will bite too:

Mr. M: (secretly wanting 15 test questions) "Great job today. Tomorrow on the test there are 30 questions."

Students: "Aw man. Thirty problems? Come on. That's so much!"

Mr. M: "Ok relax. How many should you have to do?"

Students: "Zero."

Mr. M: "Zero is not happening. Say zero again we go back to 30. I can live with 25."

Students: "No way that's still too many. Five."

Mr. M: "I want 30; you want zero. I want 25; you want five. I will live with 15. Don't forget how nice I am." If they don't complain, I get more than I want. Negotiating is a skill rarely taught or practiced in school. I like when students do it. It makes them feel empowered, gets results, and usually costs us nothing.

CHAPTER 2

~

The Real Problems

There are seven reasons kids misbehave, but I believe the first five are most important. Please hold up your hand and look at all five fingers. Place your hand on your chest with your palm down and your fingers up. Imagine that each finger represents a pipe to a well-hydrated person. Well-hydrated equals well behaved. Students filled in all five are very well behaved. Four of five are very well behaved. Three of five are well behaved. Two of five are fence kids. A fence kid = when X is absent Y behaves. If X is here Y is a disaster. Y is the fence kid. He goes whichever direction pulled. One of five exhibits some difficult behavior every day. Zero of five are the high flyers, the ones who take most of our time and often disrupt learning for everyone else.

Let's Examine These Five More Closely:
Attention: Grab your thumb and don't let go. The thumb represents the need for attention. Attention seeking is so prevalent and such a part of why kids misbehave it lives alone. It is sort of like the RA of the dorm. There are two types of "attention" kids. Attention "A" stereotype has six brothers and sisters in a single parent home. Parent often has a boyfriend or girlfriend. The student craves more attention because he gets very little outside school. Attention "B" gets so much attention at home she struggles without it. You call mom to explain what happened and she immediately says, "That's not what my daughter says! She says you're

the problem and she never lies to me! I just love her so much." At home mom says come in for dinner at five. Daughter comes at seven. Mom says, "Here is your dinner, honey, and I will clean up for you too because I love you so much." Daughter now comes to school and we tell her to wait in line and take turns. Notice "attention" is the problem for both but the solution is completely different. Attention "A" needs more while attention B needs less.

Power / Control: The pointer and middle fingers represent power and control. These kids love to argue. We tell them to sit. They stand because we tell them to sit.

We say, "Wow it is so nice outside."

They say, "No! It's beautiful."

We say, "Right that's what I said."

They say, "No. You said nice and it's beautiful. They are two totally different things." These kids make us wonder where the last ten minutes of life went. Generally, their life is out of control in one of two ways: They are overly controlled at home or allowed to do whatever they want. For some, every detail of every day is mapped out by overbearing parents. This student is often bossed around or even abused at home, thus feeling very little power / control. Others are allowed to do whatever they want with very little supervision at home. Both ends of the spectrum leave a student "dehydrated." Schools, in general, are not set up for kids to feel power and control. We control everything: Rules, consequences, homework, when to eat, how to dress, when to use the bathroom, schedules, what is on the test. I could go on. Most students in most classes do not get power and control in school, but they still do not disrupt because they get that need filled somewhere else in life. A small percentage of kids get none, anywhere. When these students are constantly told, they rebel against authority to prove they can. When traced back, almost always Oppositional Defiant kids are desperate for power and control.

6

Competence: The ring finger represents competence. Some kids are naturally good at school. They sit still, pay attention, follow directions, memorize, and read really well. Success, confidence, and competence are breeders of each other. Being successful leads to confidence, which eventually leads to competence. The more competent, the more success someone has and the more confident he becomes. I am reminded of this cycle more than ever right now as I am coaching my son's tee ball team. The ball goes on a tee. This is not baseball. Real baseball does not involve a tee. We use it anyway because success comes first. Next we graduate to underhand coach pitch. To be clear, as the coach pitcher, I am not trying to throw a strike. I am literally trying to hit the bat! Success leads to confidence leading to competence. The process continues at a different pace for each kid based on natural ability and work ethic. Eventually (I am thinking a couple years still) the kid says, "Coach / Dad, throw it harder. You are not throwing it hard enough. I know I can hit it but you have to move back and throw it harder." Some kids never had math on a tee, and we throw them 90 mile per hour fastballs every day. Of course they want to quit.

Belonging: The pinky represents belonging. Like attention, there are two types of belonging kids. The stereotypical loner without many friends is Belonging "A." Belonging "B" is the kid who takes on the system. I know Belonging "B" very well, because that is who I was in Mrs. Mills' class. I still recall an incident with my 4th grade classmate, Edwina. She was a rare student, friendly with everyone. One afternoon I saw a silhouette of Edwina and Mrs. Mills arguing. Edwina stormed back to her seat and put her head down. I whispered, "Hey, are you ok?"
Her: (with tears) "No."
Me: "Well tell her she's a b*tch."
Her: "Are you crazy? I'm not saying that to a teacher!"
Me: "Want me to say it for you?"
Her: (wide eyed and smiling) "Yes!"

7

Me: (in front of the whole class) "Hey! You are going to make Edwina cry? She is the nicest kid in the whole school! You're a b*tch!" The whole class erupted in laughter. I belonged! The problem was my entire sense of belonging was tied to taking on the system. My whole life people said, "Wait until Brian comes; he will say it. Get Brian he will do it. Brian will buy it. Brian will sell it. Brian will try it." This student need is why privacy matters so much. Talk to kids in their ears. Get them away from friends. Drop a quick note and use eye contact to get your point across. The goal is to make students feel like they belong.

Awareness: Occasionally, the student is literally unaware of the behavior. Kids who tap their pens fit in this category. Sometimes the tapping actually focuses the student. When asking awareness kids to stop generally they do and often even apologize. 30 seconds later, they tap again. These kids often just need a replacement behavior. Let them tap the pen on a carpet square; kid gets the need filled without bothering anyone else.

Need to Look "Cool" in Front of Their Friends: The audience plays a role in every performance. If peers are watching, expect certain students to challenge authority every time. Kids must look cool in front of each other. It has always been this way and always will be. The second to last word is almost always best. Remember, anytime you want to deliver a message to a student and others can hear, there is a good chance a power struggle will occur.

Concluding Thought: With the toughest kids, focus on giving as much attention, power, control, competence and belonging as possible. These words are always the foundation of behavior change. Academics are the kitchen or bathroom. Without a strong foundation the most beautiful bathroom crumbles every time.

CHAPTER 3

~

It is All About Relationships

The most important (and hardest to grasp) concept learned in recovery is every time I have a problem in my life I am part of the cause. Before recovery, I believed everyone else was the problem. Failing a test or class was the teacher's fault. Getting cut from a team was the coach's fault. If a girl didn't like me she was clueless (ok I guess that's true). I never understood or believed I had the power to change my own behavior to improve outcomes. With this in mind, think about the relationships in your life with the toughest kids (or adults). How can you change to repair them? Have you called suspended students at home? Have you spent your own lunch with your toughest kids listening to them? Have you modified assignments to ensure success? Have you apologized to a student for the part you played in a power struggle? The term "build relationships" has become cliché. Telling the average person to build relationships with a challenging student is like telling the average author to build a house. I don't know how to build a house. What happens first? What comes next? How long does a house take to build? What should I expect during the process? Aren't there different kinds of houses? Do all require exactly the same steps to build? Do I build this house during my normal workday or my own time?

Places to Build:

- In class when the student is in our class.
- In school when the student is not in our class.
- Outside of school. This includes any place outside or off school grounds plus phone calls, texts, and social media.

In Class: My former principal requires us to greet students at the door. We have to stand straight up with arms folded across chest. We are allowed to high five, fist bump, or handshake as well. We have to keep one foot in the room and the other in the hallway. Smiling is always required. In this position we do three things without moving. We say, "Good morning" to a student walking in, quickly tell those in the room to settle down, and hurry those in the hallway to class. Smiling shows I am inviting and arms crossed shows authority. If all staff in the building position this way almost nothing is missed. I recall one time when I was not at the door and my principal stopped in my room. From behind, I felt a tug on my ear:

Her: "Hi Brian. Are you a bad teacher? Bad teachers stand behind their desks when kids walk in. Good teachers stand at the door. Do you understand why I care so much about this so much?"

Me: "Honestly, no. I think you are kind of a lunatic." (I don't recommend saying this to your administrator).

Her: "It does not matter what you plan over there (points to my desk) if you are not over here when they walk in. Your lesson begins when kids walk through that door. Look in their eyes. Have they eaten? Do they need a shower? Are they exhausted?" For most teachers, greeting kids means a quick hello while ushering them into the room. For some kids, it is a chance to connect on a personal level. The door greeting should include a mix of spoken observations, questions, compliments, and quick reminders. Greetings are about one or two seconds per student. The goal is to gain information for later use:

- "What's up Eli? You look tired. What time you go to bed last night? Who was home with you?"
- "Hey Brookie. I saw some of your game. You were fantastic. Don't forget we have a Science Club meeting today after school. Please be on time!"
- "Tommy. Love the new shirt. That color looks awesome on you. All good with your girlfriend?"

Jot down or make mental notes of who needs more attention later. Look for sadness, baggy eyes, torn clothes and messy hair. Let kids talk for a few minutes before class. Instead of telling them to quiet down, listen closely for a nugget to turn into a lesson. This is not the time to get into long discussions (unless you have a paraprofessional, co-teacher or student teacher).

Tell Students About You: I model this for you in the first few pages. Reading struggles, removed from school with no warning, severe ADHD, on medication, and in addiction recovery. I take the dirtiest of my laundry and dump it in your laps because it hooks you. It makes you say, "I want to read more from this guy." We want kids to open up, but often don't give much back. Let them know your likes and dislikes. Tell them your strengths. Explain the struggles you've overcome to succeed in your life. Opening up gives them courage to do so in return.

"I'm Good At" Board: Ask elementary kids to bring a picture of them from that summer doing one thing they are good at. It can be anything. Riding a bike, playing catch with your dad, and riding a skateboard are examples. On the first day of school each student is given two note cards pre-labeled, "In School" and "Out of School." Each writes one activity they are good at in each place. It does not have to match the picture, but often does. Pictures are hung on the board and note cards are tacked under each picture. Think of it like Facebook, which is the big thing. Inside the big thing everyone gets his / her own little world. Students now know who to ask if struggling in a certain area of school. It also allows us to connect with kids on a personal level, building climate and culture in a school. The "I'm good at board" is great for new students during the school year. Before introducing the person to the class, have her pick two or three names off the board over common interests. The teacher introduces the new student to those selected students only. They introduce her to everyone else.

Criticism or Abuse: The best staff meeting I ever attended had the word "CRITICISM" in bold letters on the screen. My principal said, "You see that word? That word matters. You must be willing to criticize kids. If you are not willing to criticize kids they can't get better. You also must be willing to accept criticism. If you are unwilling to accept criticism you can't get better." Then she pushed a button on her computer and the word "compliment" came flying into the screen about 100 times surrounding the word criticism. She said, "Don't ever forget criticism on its own, left unaccompanied by compliment, is not criticism it is abuse. There are certain kids in this school being abused every day. We don't mean to do so, but they go from your class to yours to yours to yours and they get criticized, criticized, and criticized again. We all have to be better."

The Uber of Information: I travel a lot, and it used to be awful. Land in a city late at night. Find the rental car counter. Stand in line. Walk to the car. Fumble with an unfamiliar navigation system while car is warming. Drive to a hotel in an unfamiliar city. Pay money to park. Drag my luggage across a parking lot (usually freezing cold), up stairs, and finally into the hotel. Repeat next morning to the school. I blocked extra time to stop for gas, car return, and shuttling back to the airport.

Once in the hotel I ate delivered pizza or hotel restaurant food. Today, I land in a city and open Uber. I type the first 3 letters of my hotel and a list pops up. I select my choice. Seconds later a name with picture, car make, model, and exact location pops up. Each driver is screened. Their driving is rated every trip. They are forbidden to look at their phones when driving. The driver meets me at the front door (or any other place I choose), in a warm car. Almost always they have short cuts to a location. As the driver pulls away, I open Uber Eats or Grubhub. During the ride I type the first three letters of the hotel name in the app. A list of restaurants, all with many customer ratings and reviews pop up. In one click I filter for exactly what I want. Two or 50 (depending on the city) choices, all with menus and exact time food will be delivered to my door. I watch, in real time, the driver pick up my food from the restaurant and see where they are in the delivery process. I finish my ride to the hotel answering emails, updating social media, or face timing with my kids and wife. I am dropped at the front door of the hotel and driver usually takes my luggage out. I try timing it so the food arrives 10 minutes after me. We live in a delivery and convenience-based world where we want what we want when we want it. Kids are no different. Great teachers are Ubers of information. We deliver math, science, social studies, or please and thank you. It does not matter how smart we are if we can't get the intelligence into the brain of a 12-year-old with limited or no parenting, who hasn't eaten or showered that day. Relationships matter because if we don't know our kids we can't design the lesson to fit their interests. Traditional lesson plans with formative evaluation, summative evaluation, and procedures require teachers create the lesson and expect students to metaphorically step into our world to learn it. This is fine with kids already excited about learning. Some kids need more. The lesson must be delivered to their door. I recommend listing student interests on one sheet of paper. Another lists lesson objectives. Planning time is spent fitting objectives to interests. If the two do not connect tell the kids, "Sometimes all of us do things in life that make no sense. There is no real reason to know this right now. So let's just battle through it."

Privacy Matters (use P.E.P.): P.E.P. stands for privacy, eye contact, and proximity. Privacy is most important, proximity is second most, and eye contact least important. I believe publicly praising people often embarrasses them the same as publicly correcting. Publicly praising one student often annoys others. Publicly correcting usually prompts defensiveness from the corrected. When using P.E.P. get as close to the student as possible, make quick and direct eye contact (if possible as you are walking over), and deliver a message into the student's ear (turn your head away from the student and talk to the back of his head). In some schools and cultures eye contact is not necessary. Focus on privacy and proximity. As soon as the message is spoken, get out of there. Do not stick around for a response. When used properly, a teacher can compliment and correct two different students within seconds of each other. Tell your class, "Sometimes I will deliver messages that are only for individual ears. I will drop by your ear as much as everyone else's. Please do not wonder what I said to that person because the message is between us." Speak quickly, directly, and firmly; then move right into something else. Always expect a mumble. Think of it as a hit and run. The movement part is so important to making this work. I love using the audience for examples and role-plays during workshops. Because of this I often invade personal space. Keeping hands in pockets ensures I do not make physical contact with a participant/student. When people get animated and upset their hands tend to flail. By keeping them in pockets, the movement is controlled.

Make Time for Student Issues: Scramble letters in the word listen and you get silent. Rhetorical question. When is the last time you sat down with your toughest kid and listened to him or her? With no expectation: not trying to get something from them or change something about them. Simply listen to them. Tell your class there will be times

14

you will sit and listen to their conversations. Set clear and firm guidelines that after a predetermined amount of time the lesson will start. I prefer the first few minutes because students enjoy talking to each other during this time anyway. Plus, I can listen for a nugget to turn into a lesson. Sometimes I use the first 10 minutes to lead a discussion about an issue I know is relevant to them, or teach a life skill they need. Last week I consulted in a middle school outside of Omaha. I said hello to 56 different students. Four of them responded appropriately by making eye contact, smiling, or shaking my hand. 52 greeted me with a version of, "Sup. Who are you? Why are you here? Are you her husband?" All okay questions, but not for an adult you've never met. If I were a full time teacher in this school, I would focus on greeting adults until perfection. I recall my former student Carol saying to me, "You have no idea what it is like to go home to paid employees every day. I don't have a mom or a dad. I live in a group home. So whatever with your English homework." Here are a few discussion topics and my number one point:

- **Bullying:** Everyone in a school is a bully, the bullied, or a bystander. Explain each and show how complacency is as bad as being the bully.
- **Social Media:** There is no such thing as 'delete.' Send or post is forever. If you have to think about it the answer is no.
- **Job Interviewing:** Teach kids to share their struggles and how they work to overcome them. Turn the mundane or boring into the extraordinary. The best example of this is from a girl named Hannah. Her interview was for a job at my ice cream store.
  Me: "Why should I hire you?"
  Hannah: "Probably you shouldn't. I mean I've never had a real job where you have to punch in and stuff. I have been a babysitter. This means there are people willing to trust me alone with the most valuable things they have. If you hire me,

I will treat your store the same way I treat those kids when you are not there. If you are willing to teach me how to work you will only have to tell me something once. I promise."

She is one of two kids in seven years we hired on the spot. The other fit into our mascot costume and we were desperate.

- **Constant Adult Fighting at Home:** Get the student a pair of headphones. At least they can tune it out.
- **Discuss goals:** Focus on one step at a time to reach them.

View this time as an investment in the same way you put money away now with the goal being worth more in the future. We add during the ups and downs trusting the process of compound interest and growth.

Teach Leadership: Ever played metaphorical whack-a-mole? In other words, the whole class is disruptive and each time one falls another pops up. Find the leaders. Stand over them and nobody else (metaphorically). Get them on your side and they will influence others. Realize that you need him more than he needs you. If you are not sure who the leader is look for:

- After giving a request, who does everyone look at?
- Who publicly seeks justice for others?
- Who are the kids that have courage?
- Who are the kids with incredible talent?
- Who tells people what to do already?
- Who acts like the bully?

Two by Ten (2 x 10): First, get the rest of the class started on a project, test, quiz, or homework assignment. As they work independently, wander to the student you need to speak with. This is a great time to ask a private question or to find out more about his or her life. Two stands for two consecutive minutes, ten for ten consecutive days. The goal to build a relationship with a student that rarely participates. Here is how it goes:

- Get the class started on a group activity, tests, quiz, or silent reading.
- Approach the student from the side.
- Get down to his or her level (or slightly below).
- Begin the conversation in as quiet and calm a voice as possible.
- Make an observation and ask a question.
- Pause three seconds waiting for a reply.
- If no response answer your own question.
- Repeat for two minutes.

Below is the 2x10 in Action:

Mr. M: "Hey man you look tired, are you?"

Tony: (No response).

Mr. M: (three second pause) "Sometimes I am tired and they pay me! If you could be anywhere else in the world right now where would it be?"

Tony: (shrugs shoulders no response).

Mr. M: "I'd pick Jamaica. I went there last year with my family and it was amazing! Have you ever been anywhere fun with your family?"

Tony: "No."

Mr. M: "If there are two things I can do to improve this class for you what are they?"

Tony: (rolls eyes). (No response).

Mr. M: "When I was your age I would say, 'never anymore tests or homework.' What do you think?"

Tony: (looking away) (No response).

Mr. M: "I am glad you do not think anything of it because I can't do either. But you can help me write the next test. What do you think about that? You can't fail a test you helped write, can you?"

Tony: (grunts)

Mr. M: "I really like your shoes they are amazing. Where did you get them?" This dialogue lasts two minutes. When Tony does not answer, I answer my question. The definition of the word "relationship" in my class is, "I learn about you and you learn about me." Many teachers want kids to open up without reciprocating. Would your relationship at home work well if you learned all about your spouse, but they got nothing back? With certain kids be prepared to converse with yourself the entire time as some will not answer no matter the question. Fortunately, most students will respond after a few questions. If I am unsure where to start: sports, music, video games, money, animals, and art. Push to find out what he likes, what his home life is like, what his interests outside of school are. If he does not respond, tell him yours. With this knowledge it is easier to work with him in the future. Remember, only two minutes. Sometimes with certain kids I start with one minute.

Get Out of my Face: Occasionally a student tells me to get out of his or her face. I always do. Actually that's a pretty good rule for anyone anywhere. My last words to the student are, "Ok. But you know I will be back." It is important he knows I am not intimidated and plan to continue this later. Sometimes other students want to know what we talked about. Remind them, "There will be many times I have private, individual conversations with different people in this class. Sometimes it will be to correct behavior, other times praising something you do well. Occasionally it will be to chat about life or ask your advice. When this happens I will not share with anyone else what we talk about. The conversation remains between the individual student and me. I promise to drop by your desk/table/area as often as your neighbor." After a few reminders they quickly learn this is how our classroom works and stop asking.

Out of Class In-school Relationship Building: Jayvan frequently disrupted my class. I began pulling him from other classes every day (most teachers never minded). We walked around the school shoulder-to-shoulder (it might be shoulder to knee depending on the age) and talked for eight to ten minutes. At first my only rule was we were not allowed to talk about school. Anything else was allowed. He could ask anything about me and I about him. Answering was always optional for both of us. I learned about an uncle who had sexually abused him three years prior. I learned he really does not like misbehaving, but he feels it is his identity. He learned about my struggles in school as a kid. Take time outside of class to get to know kids and incredible things happen. My favorite relationship building spots in a school:

- Hallways between classes (middle and high school).
- Student Cafeteria (all grades).
- Recess (elementary).
- Bus loop when students are entering and leaving (all grades).
- Library (all grades).
- Gym (all grades).
- Art Room (all grades).
- Music Room (all grades).
- After school clubs (all grades).

Hallways: Occasionally connect with kids in noisy places as controlled chaos also offers privacy. Be visible in the hallway between classes. Observe student interactions. Say hello to and ask one question of as many students as possible. The noise and mass movement make it perfect for private conversation. If not sure what to say give a compliment or ask for advice. Make a commitment to doing this at least one time every day with the same student.

Student Cafeteria: Obnoxiously loud environments are perfect for private conversation. Stand at a distance and observe class dynamics. Usually when observing I prefer that students not see me. Ask individual kids to walk with you for a few minutes. Start the conversation by reminding it is your lunch. "Right now I can do many other things, but I am concerned about you. In fact, I am giving up my lunch to figure out what's going on. Can you please fill me in?" When kids see that you are willing to work with them on your own time the relationship becomes stronger. The student cafeteria is a great place to meet students we do not teach. Plus, lunch monitors and cafeteria crew always appreciate our help.

Recess: I can't say this any more clearly: unless safety is the reason, do not take recess away from kids. If anything, add more recess. Start a game or activity with a group. A few minutes later let someone fill in. Start another game with a different group. Then jump to another. Have one-on-one chats with a student or small group. After chatting jump back to the game. Chat during the game. Have a sign-up sheet available for students that want to talk. Set time limits, as a few will try dominating your every moment.

Library: It is rare to find a quiet public place. Libraries are the exception in most schools. I met a librarian in Hawaii who created an "adopt a shelf" program. Each student in the school has a shelf they are responsible for organizing.

The Bus: I challenge each elementary teacher to ride the bus home from school with every student one time. Middle and high school teachers pick 10 different kids and do the same. At school, greet buses in the morning. Smile and say hello to students as they get off. Stand outside when they leave. Have quick conversations. Remind some about homework, wish others good luck in games, or offer some advice for a tough home life. Occasionally, invite the bus driver into class to teach a lesson or help an individual student.

Outside of School Relationship Building: I mentioned earlier coaching my son's tee ball team. I love running around with the kids and acting silly. Even if you can't coach, attend as many games, plays, and recitals as possible. These events help tremendously when connecting with tough kids. Let them see you in a hooded sweatshirt, jeans, and a hat. One of my students works at my dry cleaner, two at a restaurant I frequent. Remember, it is more important to be seen than it is to see. Arrive a few minutes before the event starts find your student(s) and make sure he or she sees you. Personally greet each if possible. Make eye contact, wave, or nod. I attended many basketball games and watched warm-ups. The ball tossed and I took off. The next day, talk to him about the game and how he did. Just be sure and check the final score first. Showing up at the end is okay, too. Be sure not to leave until you are positive the student sees you. Usually administrators attend school events. Be sure they see you too. Make eye contact, wave, personally greet them, and always introduce guests. Administrators think I am at every event. I have a letter of recommendation from a former principal that says, "Brian is at everything. He is ultra-involved in their lives, especially outside of school. I don't know how he does it!" Now she knows.

Other Outside of School Relationship Building Places:

- Volunteer in a soup kitchen or homeless shelter.
- Ask them to attend your events outside of school (I play golf, softball and volunteer with Special Olympics and Big Brothers Big Sisters).
- Do a home visit. Get parental permission and be sure another adult is home and present in the room at all times.
- Skype / Facetime absent kids.

Invite Them Over? There are dozens of reasons not to invite students over which is why a well conceived invite, to a proper social situation, is an exceptionally meaningful moment in the life of a child. It is also an effective behavior management strategy. Liz lived in a group home. Holidays were especially difficult for her. As Thanksgiving approached I expressed sadness to my family that Liz had nobody special to share the holiday with. My mom, who was a teacher for 27 years, suggested I invite her for Thanksgiving dinner with our family. Arrangements were made for a caseworker from the group home to drive her, stay for dinner, and bring her home. There were about 20 people at my house that night. Liz sat next to my mom. She was perfectly well behaved and even helped clean dishes. She never disrupted my class again and once yelled for everyone to, "shut the f*ck up! Mr. Mendler is trying to teach!"

He is Suspended and I can Build a Relationship: A teacher recently said to me, "This week we were on break and the week before he was suspended. Tomorrow he comes back. What do I do?" My answer, "Too late. It is not what you do when he comes back. What did you do while he was gone? Did you call and say, 'I know you are suspended but I wish you weren't. To me you are an important part of our class / school and at least one person will miss you while gone. If you don't want to be further behind please let me know. If a parent or guardian is home I will bring work to your house. If they stay I might too and help you do it. If not, no big deal I just want you to know how much I care. Have a great day." This call takes less than a minute. The student comes back from suspension with a hat on in the hall. A teacher tells him to take it off and he tells her where to stick it. You tell him to take it off he says, "Sorry, sir." It has nothing to do with the hat and everything to do with when the student was in trouble, one teacher washed her hands of the student, but you reached out to help. If you teach the suspended student, make it your goal is to call him every night he is out. If you do not teach the suspended student, every other night is the goal.

Other Relationship Building Phrases:

- "You are my hero. What you've been through in your life would make most people quit. You keep coming back. I am so grateful and proud I get to teach you!"

- "I saw your (fill in the blank). I really liked it."
- "When I was your age, I did that too. Don't worry. Want to know how I fixed it?"
- "I like your (fill in the blank). Where did you get it?"
- "Do you know they follow you? You're a great leader."
- "Can you please help me with (fill in the blank)?"

Calling to Correct Starts with Something Positive: Think of a sponge. In order to absorb it must be softened. Parents are no different. When calling home start with something positive. For example:

Mr. M: "Hi Mrs. Smith. This is Mr. Mendler. How are you?"

Mrs. S: "I'm not sure."

Mr. M: "Please know Derrick is one of the most assertive people I know. He is never afraid to speak his mind. Overall, that is a good thing. He is also a leader and has ability to influence others. They follow, listen to, and often do what he says. I love these qualities and will continue to mold them in a positive way. Occasionally, he leads negatively. I do not believe it is intentional, but I would like to give you an example that happened today. I noticed he along with two others told Frank, a new boy in our class, not to sit with them at lunch. I am positive he will be a major force in this class helping to prevent bullying in the future. Are you interested in helping turn his leadership positive?"

Mrs. S: "How can I help?"

Mr. M: "Start by commending your son on being a leader. Tell him I called to say how many good qualities he has. Explain it is important he lead in a positive way. Tell him that you (mom) were sometimes picked on in school and it made you feel awful. Explain how you wished there was someone like him in your class that was courageous enough to help. Then, ask if bullying happens in his class. He might say no and ask if I said he was a bully. Tell him I said sometimes I think he can utilize his leadership skills in a better way, but overall I am really proud of him. Then ask if you can count on him to help stop any bullying he sees."

Analyzing this Conversation: I pick the word "assertive" to describe Derrick. I tell his mom he is a leader and willing to speak his mind. These are both excellent qualities. By softening her with positives, mom is more likely to absorb ideas, suggestions and corrections. I mention Derrick influences others in a negative way. Then I give a specific example. Everything is phrased as non-threatening as possible. I never call Derrick a bully. Instead, I explain how he "influences" others. I tell Mrs. S. "we" can help get it to stop. This gets her to ask what she can do. Remember, many parents have no idea what to do. Give specific suggestions. Then I ask Derrick's mom to tell her son she was picked on when younger in school. The goal is for Derrick to think of his mother every time he excludes others. It is helpful to give parents two or three specific strategies to help with what the phone call is about. Try making at least two positive calls or texts per week to parents of difficult students. Do not tell the student ahead of time. Often a surprise Monday night call to praise hard work, leadership or teamwork will produce good behavior for the rest of the week. Thank the parent for doing a fine job at home with their son or daughter. This goes a long way toward gaining parental support in the future.

The Perfect Newsletter: My son's teacher, Mrs. Pylko, has five children of her own at home. We still get a detailed newsletter every Saturday by noon. An example follows not to scare you, but to show what you are competing with.

Hello Friends,

Many of our tadpoles were becoming froglets so we knew it was time to set them free. We walked down the path and let them go where we do every year in a small (water collection) pond. The children loved to check on the tadpoles every morning upon arrival to see how fast they were growing and changing.

Once again the children were busy baking. This time they made Father's Day jumbo muffins. They made our usual banana bread recipe that we have set out as a work. To make them "fancy" for Father's day the children could choose to add chocolate chips and sprinkles.

We read, "Weaving a Rainbow" by George Ella Lyon, which inspired several of the children to do some paper weaving. We also read some new Gerald and Piggy books. We almost have the complete set. The children love to listen to these books again and again.

The children did very well for our emergency drill this week. We had a verbal "alarm" so there wasn't the startling fire alarm. We lined up quickly and then walked over to St. Bernards. The drill went smoothly and when we came back to the classroom everyone had some cold water to drink and we answered any of their questions about the whole process of both our emergency drills and fire drills.

Our phonogram of the week is "ch." Thank you Karen for sharing your Dad. He read the books The Boy Who Drew Birds, a Story of John James Audubon" by Jaqueline Davies and "Calvin Can't Fly" by Jennifer Berne. He and Karen also showed some pictures of the bird's nest at their house with eggs and then baby birds. Karen's Dad also read a Gerald and Piggy book "The Thank You Book" by Mo Willems.

Thank you to Mr. B. and Mrs. K. for helping the children make their meditation bottles. This is a spring tradition in our classroom. The children then have something to focus on when they practice making silence. Plus they are so sparkly and pretty. Some of the afternoon friends had them outside in the sunshine and they were so beautiful.

Have a great weekend,
Mrs. Pylko

I Believe Every Child is Gifted and Talented: Some require more searching than others. Jeff entered my self-contained class midway through the year. His grades were disastrous and his basic reading and writing skills were well below average. One day he dropped his notebook and out spilled some of the most spectacular drawings and sketches I'd ever seen. Jeff told me he never took a drawing or art class. Later that day I facilitated a meeting between him and the art teacher.

Concluding Thought: Relationships always come first with the toughest kids. Students will follow us if we take extra time to know them as people. Ask yourself: Why did I go into teaching in the first place? For me it is to change lives. Focus on the people in front of you. Kids always come before content. My students as people come first and my students as learners second. Emphasize individual strengths. Is someone a frustrated reader but great speaker? Is someone else a struggling listener but great leader? Sometimes it is hard to find student strengths. Emphasize them and set up situations in class for students to utilize what they are good at.

CHAPTER 4

~

That's Not Fair

Thankfully I learned this concept early in my career. I always understood to differentiate homework, consequences, tests, quizzes, and assignments based on individual student needs. I did not know how to respond or what to do when one student complained about what I did for someone else. First the teacher must commit to not talking about what he/she is doing for one student to any other student. Just like doctors do not discuss individual patient medication with other patients, teachers should not discuss one child's consequence, homework, grade, bathroom break, or classroom seat, with any others. This goes for parents too. No matter how hard a student or parent tries getting me to talk about another student I will not. I say this to my class early in the school year. "Fair in this classroom means every person always gets what is needed for success. Equal means everyone gets the same thing." If I have 25 different minds 25 different thoughts 25 different feelings and 25 home lives I can't treat them all the same way. I suggest every teacher write the word *fair* and the word *equal* in a prominent location. Then laminate the definitions of each. Say, "I am going to make a promise you will love me for. I promise always to do my best to be *fair* to each of you, which means I will not always treat you the same way. Some of you might get different assignments, consequences, tests, etc... When this happens please do not complain I am not being fair."

Student: "I have to write a whole essay and she gets to write one paragraph? That's not fair."

Teacher: "What is the problem with your assignment? I believe you are an excellent writer and can easily complete an entire essay."

Student: "My friend only has to write one paragraph."

Teacher: "I understand what she is doing. What is the problem with your assignment?"

Student: "I told you. My friend only has to write one paragraph. It is not fair."

Teacher: "Just like I would never discuss your work with another student I am not discussing other people's work with you. When you are ready to talk about your work I am glad to listen." Then walk away.

In baseball the saying is, "Three strikes and you're out." Here it is, "Three strikes and I am out." Strike one, the student talks about her friend. I correct her by politely reminding I am willing to discuss only her work. Strike two she talks about her friend again. A little less politely I correct her with another invitation to discuss her work. Strike three she talks about her friend a final time. I calmly and firmly say, "When you are ready to talk about your work (test, consequence, etc...), I am glad to listen." Then, I walk away like a boss. Like I own the room and later today I might close on the room across the hall. Remember the student might mumble grumble about you under her breath. Keep walking. Don't be the helpless fish and get hooked into a power struggle. Some kids will tell you about a problem with another student. If this happens, first teach students to own the problem. "Mr. Mendler, I feel scared. I believe if I go on my bus today I am going to get beat up. Can you please help?" The student does not complain about someone else. Now you can figure out who needs to get involved to keep this student safe. When safety is an issue, kids must feel the school is doing everything possible to protect them.

Consistency: Simply says we do the same thing not what that thing is. Consistently be fair. Consistently stop worrying about treating everyone the same way. Consistently give each student what she needs to succeed. Consistently do not talk to one about what you do for another. Consistently make decisions based on what is best for each individual. Consistently talk to parents about only their child. Consistently focus on five reasons kids misbehave when meeting about them. Consistently praise and correct as privately as possible. Consistently be a second to last word person. The general concept of consistency works because most eight year-olds read at a third grade level. Most 16 year olds read at a 10th or 11th grade level. For most kids, in most situations, *equal* is *fair*. It just is not always the case. The third grader reading at a sixth grade level and sixth grader reading at third grade level each get what is needed without others complaining. Here, fair could never be equal.

Ten Responses for Kids who Complain:

- "I will always try to be fair. I will not always treat you the same way."
- "Different people might get different assignments, tests, or consequences. Please do not complain it is not fair."
- "I appreciate the concern about your friend. What is the problem with what I did for you?"
- "When you are ready to talk about you, I am glad to listen."
- "It is fair. It is not equal. Please remember the difference."
- "I am available until 'this' time. If you have a better idea I am glad to hear. Until then I must do what I think best. I look forward to hearing from you."
- "I realize she did not raise her hand. Thank you for raising yours every time."
- "Thanks for worrying about her grade. I am sure she

appreciates it. Can you please tell the problem with your grade?"

- "I appreciate you noticing he needs more time. Are you saying you need more time?"
- "Thanks for noticing his head is down. I appreciate you keeping your head up."

Ten Responses to Practice for Parents who Complain:

- "I am always open to hearing a better solution for your child. Please do not complain about what I do for other people's children."
- "I promise never to discuss your son or daughter behind your back with another parent."
- "This means I can not discuss other children with you unless their parents are present."
- "Thanks for your concern. Is there problem with what I did for your son / daughter?"
- "Unfortunately, I cannot discuss why her friend gets extended time. Fortunately, your daughter does not need extended time. She finished early."
- "I do not care about the consequence. I care about improved behavior. From now on I will call you. Thanks for the help."
- "I am sorry. Sometimes teachers make mistakes. Obviously I gave your daughter too much work. Please tell her to hand in what is complete and she is all set. Thanks for not complaining about others."
- "I am available until 4pm. If you have something better I am excited to hear. Until then I will do what I think best. I am so thankful for your concern."
- "Thanks for your concern about her friend's grade. Is there a problem with your son / daughter's grade?"
- "To me homework and consequences are vehicles to a

destination. The destination is not negotiable but the vehicle is."

Kids and parents quickly learn it is pointless to complain about others. This forces them to focus on themselves. Eventually the student says, "I don't think I should do 10 problems tonight. I have baseball practice and my grandmother's birthday party." Avoid a power struggle with, "Ok. How many will show me you understand the material?" Some kids say, "None." My response: "None is not happening (set limit). I wish it could happen (put myself on his team). Do you know how much easier my life is if I give none? I have no papers to correct or grade. I might even get to bed before midnight. Unfortunately, my principal might get annoyed. Some of your parents might wonder what I am doing every day. How about seven?" If he complains again say, "Please tell me another number and do not say 'zero' or we go back to 10." He says "two." You say, "I want 10 you want none. I want seven you want two or three. I will live with five only because I am the coolest teacher ever. Please pick the five you prefer. Tell your grandma happy birthday." Then walk away. One-size-fits-all formulas are outdated and do not work for the toughest kids. We have academically and emotionally diverse students not all capable of succeeding at the same thing in the same way on the same day at the same time. Be fair without worrying about treating everyone the same.

Concluding Thought: Administrators are helpful by staying away from school wide policies requiring all students to be treated the same way. Use the words "usually," "often," and "most of the time," when creating policies. Encourage teachers not to have one-size-fits-all mentalities. Be fair to teachers without always treating them the same way. I had a provision in my contract allowing me to miss 10 days of school to teach staff development. A few colleagues complained it was not fair. My principal should have said, "Unfortunately I am not discussing Brian's contract with you. Thank you for being here and worrying about your contract." Instead, he tried justifying which always

31

makes things worse. Do not talk to one teacher about what you are doing for another. Tell teachers your goal is to be fair, which means they will not always be treated the same. Some might have 30 students and others 27. Some might teach six periods and others five. Ask students not to complain things are not fair. Instead look at every individual situation before making a decision. My first ever staff meeting our principal said, "This is my world. I run it. Each of you runs a small country inside my world. Occasionally your country will get asked to do something for the good of the world that you don't understand. Like take on a new citizen or two. You might complain your borders are full. Trust me they are not. I am not changing the world because one country has a bad day. Faculty meetings are my time to tell you how the world is going to work. They are not your time to tell me how it should work. Because of this, they will never last more than 20 minutes. If they last more than 20 minutes you can leave, no questions asked." Then she said, "From six to seven Monday and Wednesday mornings I am in my office with the door open and light on. This is the time to tell me how to make the world better for your country to exist." I worked for that woman three straight years, set my alarm nine times, and went in once. The other eight times I woke up, looked at the ceiling and thought, "I don't care that much," hit snooze and went right back to sleep. Her rule, "If it is not worth an hour of sleep for you it is not worth my time listening." She also told us we are allowed to complain about anything if we have a solution.

CHAPTER 5

~

Creative Teaching Strategies

Last year I worked in 64 schools and visited over 200 classrooms. I did not create most of these strategies and do my best to give credit. I apologize for not always knowing the original source.

This Almost got me Fired: 24 hours before the first day of school my principal told me I was teaching one section of economics to six seniors that "can't handle a regular class. There is no state test, and you can get as creative as possible." At least that's what he said. To be clear, I have zero experience teaching economics. At the time, however, I was heavily into buying and selling on Ebay, which gave me an idea. First, I set up an account under our class name. I emailed our staff asking for any items they want to get rid of. The class then did it all. They took the pictures, wrote the descriptions, packaged and shipped the items. In return the kids got 20%. They can't wait to learn percentages. At one point my room looked like a pawnshop. This lasted until my colleagues ran out of stuff. Next, I called parents and asked them to send items. My students scoured garage sales on weekends looking for gems to resell in class. Eventually, my principal shut it down because my kids were "making too much money." He didn't want to and did everything possible to keep it alive. He also didn't know all the details. My rule is to ask forgiveness instead of permission when unsure. I am not saying this should be your rule. Each person decides this for him or herself. One student from that class is an EBAY Power Seller and makes over 40 grand a year.

Velcro and Tape: The rough side of velcro and sticky side of tape are great stimulation for kids with ADHD.

Music Stands: Politely ask to borrow one or two music stands. Tell kids who need movement to use the stand. It is height adjustable has a hard writing surface and a ledge that holds pens, pencils, and papers. If the stand is in a different part of the room it can also act as a stimulant. Kids can move between their desk and the stand, seeing the same room from a different perspective.

Multiple Seats: Recently I worked in a first grade class. Upon entering it was easy to spot the challenging student as his desk was "quarantined" from the others. During class he got out of his seat, walked to the other side of the room, and sat in a different seat. Then back to his original. After class I asked him about the seats. Our conversation:
Me: "Hey buddy. I am just curious about the two different seats. I notice you are the only one who moved during class."
Him: "My teacher says I am special. This is my home (points to the original seat) and this is my vacation home (points to the other seat). My teacher says I am allowed to go between my two homes but I can't stop at anyone else's home because that's trespassing and I could go to jail."

Carpet on the Desk: There are two kinds of pen tappers. The first taps intentionally with the goal to drive us crazy. This strategy does not work for them. The second taps because he is unaware. He often pays attention to the lesson and does not intend to disrupt. When asked to stop he does and is genuinely sorry. One day I arrived to school a bit later than normal. My paraprofessional was duct taping small squares of carpet to each desk. She asks the kids, "Who is tired of hearing Mr.

Mendler complain? Please just tap on the carpet so he stops." Her rule is the more money you make the more blame you take. She enforces rules and when students complain blames me. I blame the assistant principal, and so on.

Swimming Noodles: I saw this in a second grade class. Fidgety students swing their feet occasionally kicking the chair or student in front. Cut the noodle in half, place it at the feet of the leg swinger, and ask him to roll it with his feet. Swimming noodles are inexpensive, make little noise, and take up almost no space.

Trash Talk: My friend Marcus teaches Special Education in Rochester NY. He has a Nerf basketball hoop in his room with a trash basket beneath. A sign above reads, "Deposit Trash Talk Here!" When hearing inappropriate language he crumples a sheet of paper and throws it at the can to remind.

Stop Sign: A high school teacher in Toledo has a giant laminated stop sign on her door. Under the sign is a list of all materials students need before entering.

Songs that Teach: Teacher tube, Havefunteaching.com and Flocabulary.com are some of my favorite sites for songs.

Content: Remember to put name on work.
Tune: She'll be comin round the mountain.
Lyrics: "The first thing on my paper is my name (my name). The first thing on my paper is my name (my name). Mr. Mendler needs to know, who did this work and so, the first thing on my paper is my name (my name)."

Content: Add, subtract, multiply, divide numbers with different signs.

Tune: Row Row Row Your boat.

Lyrics (+, -): "Same sign add and keep, different sign subtract, take the sign of the highest number then you'll be exact."

(X, division): "Same sign multiply positive all the time, different signs make negatives every single time. Rules for division are same as multiply, now you are an integer whiz lets give it a try."

Content: In a Cell.

Tune: Jingle Bells.

Lyrics: "In a cell, in a cell, there is so much stuff. Cytoplasm, cell membrane, and a nucleus. In a cell, in a cell, the nucleus is in control, and outside a cell membrane, the cytoplasm holds."

Content: Water Cycle.

Tune: She'll be Comin' Round the Mountain.

Lyrics: "Water travels in a cycle yes it does (clap clap), water travels in a cycle yes it does (clap clap). It goes up as evaporation. Forms clouds as condensation. Comes down as precipitation yes it does (clap clap)."

Quotes or Inspirational Sayings on the Wall: A school I worked early in my career has a banner of positive quotes wrapping the hallways. Each quote and author stenciled into the wall in a very creative, artsy way. My first writing assignment requires each student list their top ten quotes. Paragraph one explains why you love the quote. Paragraph two what it personally means to you. Paragraph three how it applies to you or family member's life.

Some of my Favorites:

"It's not about what it is. It is about what it can become."

> **- Dr. Seuss**

"Only those who dare to fail greatly can ever achieve greatly."
   - Robert F. Kennedy

"I have taken more than 9000 shots in my career. I have lost almost 300 games. On 26 occasions I have been trusted to take the game winning shot… and missed. And I have failed over and over and over again in my life, and that is why… I succeed."
   - Michael Jordan

"Do the best you can until you know better. When you know better. Do better."
   - Maya Angelou

"We must develop and maintain the capacity to forgive. There is some good in the worst of us and some evil in the best of us. When we discover this we are less prone to hate our enemies."
   - Dr. Martin Luther King Jr.

Reminders for Adults: ABT stands for Always Be Teaching. Whatever a student does or says, always teach. If he is rude, teach how to ask for things appropriately. If she grunts when you say "hello" show her to properly greet adults. Inappropriate behavior is an opportunity to teach skills. NBP stands for Never Be Punishing. Many of our toughest kids are punished every day by life. We can't make their life worse. Instead focus on making it better.

Best for Kids: An administrator I know requires teachers to promise making every decision based on what they believe best in that moment for that child. She promises if we do this, there will always be a place for us in education even if we upset some people along the way.

QTIP = Quit Taking It Personally: Work hard to stay personally connected to kids without taking personally what they do and say. This is not easy but when mastered it changes your life with difficult people. A student says, "Mr. Mendler you are the worst teacher ever and I hate you." I say, "I hear the anger and displeasure. I am not sure why you are upset, but I am happy to listen after class. Thanks for waiting." Teacher walks away. Student mumbles. Teacher remembers second to last word person. No power struggle, situation defuses, and lesson continues. I acknowledge his feelings and give a time to finish the conversation. I thank him for waiting and walk away.

Wild Card Question: Occasionally kids over study for a test. Over study means a student studies the causes of the civil war for two hours. On the test there are only a few questions related to causes and the student becomes deflated. Often he says, "I studied the causes so much and they were barely there." Wild Card allows him to cross out one question he does not want to answer. In its place he writes a question he wishes were asked and answer it correctly.

50/50 and Ask the Teacher: A teacher in Georgia allows each student two lifelines on a test or quiz. The first is 50/50. The student chooses one multiple-choice question and the teacher crosses out two wrong answers, leaving two choices to guess from. If the student is sure it is A or B and tells you such, do not take away C and D. "Ask the Teacher" allows each student to request an answer from the teacher to a question they do not know.

Students Write Test Questions: Fills the need for attention, power, control, competence and belonging at the same time. Break the class into groups of five. Each group gets a sub topic of the unit. Using the Civil War, group one is causes, group two important battles, group three important people, group four the effects. Two days before the test each group submits eight to ten questions related to that subtopic. One teacher I know creates a teacher test and a student test. His seventh graders get five minutes to review both. Each then turns over the test he does not want to take and proceeds with the other.

Index Card: Each student crams as many notes on one note card to use on a test or quiz.

Four Question Quiz: This strategy accomplishes two goals. First, it hooks kids up with a high test or quiz grade and second it allows me to learn from them. Occasionally when my kids have a fantastic week I say, "Ok test time. Instead of 30 questions there are four.

Questions One and Two: What are two things about me as a teacher you like a lot?

Questions Three and Four: What are two things about me as a teacher you do not like? If you can press a button and change any two things, what are they and why? Some say, "We love you Mr. Mendler you are the best teacher ever. My answer, "I guess you get a 50%." Others say, "We don't like you Mr. Mendler. You are the worst teacher ever. My answer, "I guess you get a 50%." I believe no matter how much you love someone there are two things they can improve. No matter how much you dislike someone they have at least two positive qualities. Questions one and two go on note card side "A," with three and four side "B." When grading, take your time with questions one and two. Kids tell things they love I do not realize I do. I can absorb and feel good. I recall a student writing, "You don't just ask what we did last weekend. You ask a million questions. Sometimes it is annoying because you want to know so much. But usually it's cool." Read questions three and four as fast as possible. Everybody doesn't like something. Do not take it personally and do not get offended. Look for a pattern. Do 25/27 say the same thing? If yes, look closer at that specific issue. I often got the word "intimidating." One girl even wrote, "Dear Mr. Mendler, It is 2:45 on a Friday. BACK OFF!" Monday I say, "Awesome job on Friday's test. You got perfect scores. I appreciate the feedback and will continue to do things you like. I also notice some of you think I am intimidating. I prefer the word passionate. Passionate means I care. A lot. For some of you more than any adult ever has. Sometimes when people care this much voices raise, faces turn red, and veins in the neck and forehead bulge. It is not my intention to intimidate. Just like you have things to work on, so do I." Administrators can use this strategy with teachers. What are two best things about how I run this building? If you can change any two things, what are they and why?

Concluding Thought: I recall Chris approaching me in April of my second year teaching. "Mr. Mendler, here is my summer reading assignment." He has a wide eager grin on his face. My response, "You are kidding, right? Six months late? Absolutely not." Looking defeated Chris turns to leave. My co-teacher, from across the room, "Chris, Chris, Mr. Mendler is a new teacher. He does not know how to take a late paper. Hand it to me so I can show him how."

Chris: "Mr. Decamp, here is my summer reading assignment."

Mr. D: (Reaching out his right hand) "Great job. Not just a good job. Great job. I know writing is hard for you and I know you struggle with it. I believe late is better than not at all so great job getting it done. But six months late? Six months? Is your paper good?"

Chris: "Yea it's good."

Mr. D: "Really good?"

Chris: "Yea it's really pretty good."

Mr. D: "If you are the teacher and a student hands you this paper the day it is due what grade do you give it?"

Chris: "It's good but not perfect because nothings perfect. Probably a 92."

Mr. D: "Now consider it is six months late. What grade do you give it?"

Chris: (Glancing up, down, and at me) "If I am a cool teacher or an a**hole teacher?"

Mr. D: (Getting a bit upset) "I don't care you pick."

Chris: "I pick cool. Probably take off six points per month times six months that's 36 plus eight because it is not perfect so a 56. But a 56 is better for my average than a zero, right?" 56 is better than zero. The entire goal of school is to make kids better. Late work policies limit our ability for in the moment decisions. I tell kids, "You can always make up, redo, or hand in anything late. I do not encourage this because on time is better than late. That said, late is better than not at all. If late what happens is based on how hard you worked the first time. How hard did you work the second time? How was your attitude? When taking the first test did you bother others while struggling or did you struggle with grace? After the make-up work (test, quiz, lab) is complete, we will agree on a grade you deserve." This always keeps incentive alive to keep grinding and behaving. Remember, the paycheck of a teacher never changes. Good, bad, happy, glad, mad and sad. It is always the same. Creative teaching strategies help us continue to enjoy a job that is overwhelming and exhausting. Focus on having fun and continue reminding yourself why you went into teaching in the first place.

CHAPTER 6

~

Values Expectations and Consequences

A value is broad, general, and explains *why* an expectation exists. I prefer the word expectation to rule. Expectations tell exactly what to do (be on time) while rules usually tell what not to do (don't be late). Expectations must be specific and tie directly to a value. In my room I create values. For example, "Everyone has the right to feel safe." Safety is the value. The expectation is, "Hands and feet to yourself." Students do not always like or agree with them, but a well-written expectation cannot be argued. The airlines are bad at most things, but they do understand the difference between values and expectations. The number one value of every airline is safety. Based on this shoes come off through security. Seat belts fastened for take off. Seatbacks and tray tables in full, upright, locked positions. Electronic devices switched to airplane mode. The value answers why and the expectation what. When I find myself answer a student with, "Because I said so;" "Because that's the way it's always been;" or "Because that's how we do it here;" I have a faulty expectation needing adjustment. In my room, I determine values and students help create expectations.

Mr. M: "Respect is the most important value this year. Please respect each other, this place, and yourself. Based on respect please hang coats, sweatshirts, and hats before class starts. Please raise hands before calling out. Please do not interrupt someone else when they are talking." I like expectations for me as well. Based on the value of respect, I will return graded work within 48 hours. I will ask permission before posting graded work, assignments, or behavior charts. I will praise and correct as individually and privately as possible. Another important value is responsibility. "Please be responsible for yourself, this classroom and our school. Based on the value of responsibility, please bring a notebook and pen every day." Students will usually follow expectations when they make sense and when you can find a way to agree with them when they argue. I believe police officers should do this.

Officer: "Sir, here is your speeding ticket."

Driver: "The limit should be higher than 45."

Officer: "Agree. When not working I fly through here myself. Unfortunately from seven to 11pm I get paid to enforce the law not create it. If you want to get it changed call our state capitol. Have a great day." To me values are most important. For each value, I prefer one or two expectations. Invite student help when creating expectations. Try not to negotiate values. Be sure expectations tell specifically *what* to do and values answer *why* it should be done. Emphasize certain expectations each week. Once you see significant improvement, move to the next expectation. Be sure to revisit expectations at least once each month making sure they still make sense.

Consequences: The goal of a consequence is to teach a better way to behave. It is not to punish or inflict misery. Many already live in foster care or group homes. Some get beaten and are sexually abused by relatives. Their whole life is a punishment. Instead, every single day make his life a little better than before he came to you. Teach manners. Teach them that when you make a mess you can always clean it up.

Destructive / Constructive: Parents decide if their suspended child stays home or enters the destructive / constructive program. The thought behind the program is you do something destructive, you repair by doing something constructive. Instead of home suspension, a high school student is property of an elementary principal for a day. I watched a first grader who literally tore up the lunchroom spend a day helping cafeteria staff prepare, serve, and clean up. I once saw two boys paint an entire hallway. This worked so well, kids got in trouble on purpose to get in destructive/constructive. If this happens make it a reward for good behavior all week. All effective consequences involve the person helping someone or something else. Attention, power, control, competence, and belonging are all filled at the same time when people help people.

Impossible to Predetermine: Consequences are natural outcomes of behavior, making them impossible to predetermine, but they usually can be anticipated. For example, usually I speed when driving from Omaha to Sioux Falls. The speed limit is 80 but should be 100. The consequence might be I get pulled over, arrive late, and pay a fine. It also might be I get there early and save time. Point is I don't know the consequence until after the behavior.

Do you Control Policies or do Policies Control you? In fourth grade Mrs. Mills had a policy saying if we behaved all week we attended Fun Friday. I usually lost the privilege by 11am Monday morning. This gives four and a half days to figure out whom to take down with me. When policies control people, schools become bad places. Policies should be written using words like usually, mostly, frequently, and often. The final line of any well-written classroom or school policy reads, "I/ we always reserve the right to change our mind." I used to work at a high school with a policy, "Any time students fight they are suspended five days." My student, Dan, was a star basketball point guard, and also a gang member. The back-up point guard, Miguel, was in a rival gang. On the court they were friends. Off it, they didn't look at each other.

Miguel's "friends" were trying to get Dan in a fight, knowing if Dan gets a five-day suspension Miguel becomes the starter. We worked like crazy with Dan, a boy with impulse control problems and a short fuse, on staying out of fights. We role-played and discussed specifically what to say when enticed. One day, Dan walked out of my room and was shoved in the back. He turned and said, "I'm trying to stay out of trouble. I don't want to fight." He took a step away and was shoved again. He said, "I'm not fighting! I need to stay out of trouble." Walking away a third time, he was punched in back of his head and fell into a locker. Dan pushed off the locker, spun around and cracked the other kid in the jaw, knocking him cold in one punch as I arrived. Dan said, "Mr. Mendler, I tried to walk away. Twice I tried, but he pushed me twice and punched me in the back of my head. What am I supposed to do?" We watched the video cameras showing it unfolding exactly as Dan said. The basketball coach, our principal, Dan, and I sat in the office.

Principal: "I have to follow the policy so he is suspended for five days."
Coach: "You can't suspend him. If you suspend him you teach other kids to start fights. That's what they want."
Principal: "I know but it is in our policy."
Coach: "Your policy? I have this stuff in my office called whiteout. Change it!" Long story short, they suspended Dan for five days. Walking out, he looked at all three of us and said, "Just so you know I'm knocking him out right away next time. No sense getting pushed, punched, and insulted when I get suspended either way." By suspending Dan without considering circumstance, my principal unraveled all the work we did. A better fighting policy says, "Most of the time when people fight there is a five day suspension. However, every situation is looked at individually. Who starts the fight? Did anyone try walking away? What consequence will fill the need for attention, power, control, competence and belonging? Final decisions are always made by people and in all situations we reserve the right to change our minds." Now we use our policy and brain.

Many predetermined consequences look like this:

1st offense:	Warning
2nd offense:	Phone call home/Move your clip
3rd offense:	Detention
4th offense:	In school Suspension
5th offense:	Suspension

Instead, I prefer saying to my toughest kid, "Hi, my name is Mr. Mendler. The consequence system in this school will be completely ineffective for you. It will not work." If level one is always warning, you may as well hand out twenty-five free disruption coupons as the students walk in. I loved teachers like this when I was in school, because I always did my best disruption first. Then I would say, "Go ahead and warn me. Tell me I shouldn't do it again. You have to warn me. It's number one on your list." Phone call home assumes parents are not the problem. Number three is detention or time-out. In fourth grade I had detention lined up from April first through June. I used to show up every day because I couldn't remember if I was supposed to be there. Fourth was ISS. This was my favorite because I could go to school but didn't have to go to class. Plus, the coolest teacher in the school usually ran the ISS room. In high school ISS the teachers even had to bring me my work. Hotels charge extra for room service, but ISS delivered for free. When the last level was out of school suspension, my thought process was, "I have four solid disruptions until then." My fourth grade teacher loved to write our names on the board and put check marks next to them. One day she got up to write my name and I said, "Wait, wait, wait, let me do that for you." I walked to the board and wrote the name BRIAN. I took a few steps toward my seat and said, "Let me make the whole day easier for you right now." I drew about 12 check marks down the entire board next to my name. Then I said, "Did you learn that in teacher school? How to write our names and put check marks?" Once again she kicked me out and wrote me up. They gave me ISS. I told my principal, "To be clear, the rules say I am not allowed to miss class, I should not come late to class, and the consequence is I am not allowed to go to class? This place is crazy."

I Believe in Consequences: Consequences are effective when they teach better ways to behave. I am for using "time out" when the student prefers "time in." If the student does not prefer time in, time out is a reward not a consequence. I am fine with a consequence list when there is not an order. Some disruptive behaviors do not warrant a warning. Many know exactly what they are doing, do it intentionally, and I am not warning them for it. When safety is an issue I understand suspending a student. That said, suspending with no plan does our community an enormous disservice. It is like dumping my garbage on the neighbor's lawn. Most suspended students are not home composing an action plan for improving behavior. They sleep and play video games all day. The following are ways to make traditional consequences more effective:

Detention: Instruction should be the foundation of any detention room. The assigning adult and student are instructors and learners. Each tells what they can do differently next time and acknowledges how the other feels. The conversation starts by the teacher apologizing. "Richard, we got into it today and I am very sorry for calling you out in front of your friends. Sometimes I get emotional, kind of like you. Sometimes I say things I don't mean. Kind of like you. It's amazing how similar we are. Do you think there's anything you can do differently next time?" When the conversation ends, detention is over. Keeping the student longer for misery sake turns the consequence to a punishment.

In School Suspension: Since time out only works for kids who prefer time in, the goal is for ISS kids to attend academic classes. The ISS instructor should work with students on what they did wrong and what to improve in the future. It is helpful if other teachers and administrators frequent the ISS room during the day. If a student misbehaves on purpose because they like the ISS teacher, occasionally bring the instructor to class as a helper.

Suspension: My wife and I were at a fundraiser recently. Someone asked how she and I have such a great relationship. She does not even hesitate, "Oh. He travels a lot." We both laugh and agree. Sometimes people need space from each other. This is why I love the destructive/constructive program. I also like to use a colleague. I had a system with our counselor, Mr. Kilgore. If a student comes from my room to his office with the book Old Yeller in hand it means I need a 15-minute break. A bright orange pass means strangulation thoughts are going through my mind. Please hold the student longer.

I Still Don't Know What to do: Tell the student how you feel and ask what they would do in this situation. This happened a few years ago:
Mr. M: I have tried everything and you continue making inappropriate noises. I can do the same ineffective things we both know won't work. Or you can tell me what it will take to get the noises to stop.
Jessica: Just move my seat. I make noises because the two girls I sit by laugh and they are my only friends. Move my seat and I won't make noises anymore.

Concluding Thought: Expectations tell a student what to do and values answer why they do it. Consequences have two goals: Teach a better way and stop the behavior or action from happening again. The most effective consequences focus on attention, power, control, competence and belonging. Although sometimes unavoidable, they are never intended to inflict misery. Remember not to number consequences sequentially. Moving three seats for one eliminates, "You always pick on me and never anyone else." Do not care about the consequence itself.

Only care only about the outcome of the consequence. This allows students to make decisions and allows us to be flexible. If something isn't working, either change or stop. The definition of insanity is doing the same thing over and over expecting a different result. Never have consequences in stone. Add the word "other" to any consequence list and try making it the most utilized.

CHAPTER 7

~

Prevent Harmful Aggression and Bullying

The number one thing learned in addiction recovery is every time I have a problem with someone, I am a big part of the cause. I believe schools and teachers must make significant changes to the fundamental ways we operate if we are really serious about preventing aggression and bullying. Institutionalized events like rewards night, honor roll, class rankings, Fun Friday, and competitive grading systems, all contribute to overall negative school climate. My brother Jason is one year and three weeks to the day older than me. We look like brothers, walk alike, and talk alike. He has a bit more hair and I am better looking, but our brains are completely different. He graduated fourth out of 356 students in his high school graduating class. I graduated 185 out of 352. He scored 29 on the ACT. I scored 19. He went to Washington University in St. Louis on a full academic scholarship and graduated with 3.89 GPA biology and history, dual major (because one wasn't enough). I went to Fredonia State and graduated with a 2.65 GPA communications. He went to the University of Rochester completing his MD and PHD before the age of 35. I was labeled ADHD, OCD, and EBD by age 12. Today, he is one of the leading Hematology Oncology blood cancer specialists in the world. I am one of the top education consultants and staff development trainers in the world. Obviously it is possible to have vastly different school experiences and both find life success. I remember hearing many teachers say, "If you were just more like your brother. How come you are not more like your brother? Your brother didn't act like that. Jason. Jason. Jason." Marsha. Marsha. Marsha. All they ever talked about was my brother. I promise the more they told me to be like him, the harder I went the other direction. Really I was saying, "Notice me for something!" One night I was in 10th grade and my brother asked me to help him study for a Spanish test. He hadn't studied yet and needed to know 50 vocabulary words in Spanish and their English translations. He looked at the list for eight minutes and asked me to quiz him. 48/50. Five minutes he studied. I can study that list for five hours (except I can't because my Ritalin will wear off) and be happy with 25-30. Then, we get to school and he wins all the awards and rewards. Kids like me get angry, frustrated, and annoyed. It starts with the adults on stage. We can't stand them. Problem is, we feel like they don't really care. So we start disliking the other kids, including our own brothers. My brother showed up to one of my workshops a few months ago. I didn't know he was there because it was a huge auditorium and he snuck in the back where it was dark. Of course how the good lord works that day I even said, "And I hated my own brother!!!!" At the end he comes walking down the aisle. Our conversation:

Him: "Hey."

Me: "Hey. How long have you been here?"

Him: "Long enough."

Me: "Now you know how I feel."

Him: "Yeah. But you only spoke from your perspective."

Me: "It is the only perspective I have."

Him: "You make it sound like I enjoyed those nights. I was the favorite and the favorite is supposed to win. The only emotion I ever felt was relief. You think it is fun to come home from school on Monday after a unit test on Friday and mom says, 'Hey Jay. What did you get on the test?' I tell her '98.' She says, 'Great what did you get wrong?' 'Mom, I got a 98.' 'I know Jason that's great. Were you careless? Did you not pay attention? I'd like you to bring the test home so we can go over it.' You think it is fun to practice an instrument for two hours a night so you can be first chair in an orchestra or win a music award when everyone else is outside riding bikes? I promise it's not."

Me: "I don't know. That never happened to me."

Him: "It is not fun. You think I didn't know what it was doing to you? What was I supposed to do? I didn't invent the system. I just played within it."

I always knew awards nights were bad for kids like me. Apparently they were bad for kids like my brother, too. Who are they good for? We don't do things in school unless they are good for kids, right? I am not insinuating awards nights directly cause bullying or lead to school shootings. I am saying it is a piece. I remember being so angry during award ceremonies. I never thought about shooting up a school but wouldn't have objected to someone else doing it. Always pay attention to how the lowest kid feels. Think of him first when planning an activity. I am not saying not to do the activity. I am saying always think of them first and plan for how they will feel and what to do when they feel that way. The following are bold steps we can take to prevent bullying and harmful aggression:

- **Eliminate/Devalue Honor Roll**: Recently, I was on a mission to get rid of honor roll. Smart kids already know they are smart. For 17 or 18 years they are told every day (and rightfully so) that they are smart. They don't need to be on a list for it. Lower kids almost never get on the list and some start resenting those who do. I realized pretty quickly honor roll is here to stay. It is engraved in the educational fabric of America. So, I decided to add to it.

- **On a Roll:** Ever go out to eat, get your food, but it is not very good? If I don't have time to send it back I add to it. I prefer hot sauce. Some do ranch, salt or ketchup. I started this in my little self-contained class and know 56 districts using it today. "On a Roll" is for kids that are improving. Maybe they didn't get a 90 on the test, but they held the door open for someone without being asked. They picked up a piece of paper they didn't drop. Their grades are not good enough for honor roll, but they are certainly on-a-roll. The rules for On-a-Roll are, any kid can make it for anything if one adult believes they should, even if six don't.

- **Compare Students to own Previous Work:** I remember my first day of 10th grade English in Mr. John's class. He held up Christina's paper, "This is an example of an 'A' in here. When you write like her you can get one, too." I knew right then there was no chance of me getting an "A." First, I was angry with Mr. John, but quickly realized he didn't care. So I got angry with Christina instead. After all, I reasoned, it was her fault I had no shot of getting an "A" in that class. I was not nearly the writer she was and my reading skills have always been low. Preventing this type of feeling among students is very easy, yet rarely done. Tell students early in the year you will compare them to their own previous work. Explain you expect each to be a better writer today than they were yesterday. Ask them to read one more chapter today than they did yesterday. Yesterday they completed three problems. Today should be five. Approach behavior the same way. "Yesterday in class you called out six times. Today I am hoping for five or less. Thank you for keeping track."

- **Eliminate/Privatize Class Rankings:** When ranking a student first, another has to be last. I have seen top students not take advanced placement classes for fear of losing the higher ranking. If you must rank students, try hard not to tell them their ranking until after graduation. I recently had a principal ask who speaks at graduation if they stop ranking students. At his school the valedictorian gives a speech. My advice; seniors privately vote for a person they most want to hear from. As some of us know, the best speakers are not always the best students.

- **Reward Everyone in Honor of One:** Pretend you are in fourth grade and I am the teacher. I say to the class, "Hey everyone. Tom is working really hard on his behavior this week, and I am proud of him. Because of this, Tom gets ten free bonus points to add on any test or quiz. Great job Tom." Are you happy for him? Maybe you are. Some will say, "I am good every week and I don't get anything? He is good once and is rewarded?" To prevent this, instead say, "Hey everyone, I don't normally talk to you about what individual people in this class are privately working on because it is not really your business. However, occasionally I believe in praising people publicly and today belongs to Tom. Because he is so amazing, all of you get ten bonus points added to a test of your choice in honor of him. Do not thank me. I had nothing to do with it." How do you feel about Tom now? I did this when teaching fourth grade. Everyone was given an extra 20 minutes of recess in honor of Ben. I witnessed one of my top students say to him, "Great job Ben. You better behave again next week too." There is a thought in education that peer pressure is bad. Peer pressure is only bad when kids pressure each other to do the wrong thing. Peer pressure is necessary when coaching a sport. I always select (or we vote on) captains before the season. I manage them and they manage everyone else for me.

- **Modify Competitive Games:** A few years ago I co-taught in a 10th grade Social Studies class. For test review we played Jeopardy. The class was divided in two teams. Each member was required to answer a question correctly for his or her team to receive points. For some kids there was zero review going on because they were so worried about answering their question. Later that day I heard a girl say to a peer, "How did you not know that? It was so easy!" Instead, give struggling students two or three possible questions and answers to those questions ahead of time. Guarantee they will be asked one of the two. Now there is much less panic and true review can happen.

- **Use Groups, Grade Individually:** Students work together on a project or presentation, but grades are not contingent upon anyone else. If a group member is lazy or does not do his or her part there is little to no peer resentment. More on groups in chapter 12.

- **Avoid Public Award Nights:** Just recently a colleague asked who I thought should win a writing award. I told him everyone. He said they only have one award. I told him no one. For me, one winner and lots of losers is a bad ratio and usually leads to problems.

- **Focus on Power and Control:** I worked in a school that had "bully patrols" on the playground. With adult supervision the biggest bullies are put in charge of helping others.

Concluding Thought: If I fix me, I fix the problem. Learning cannot happen when students feel afraid, threatened, and intimidated. The number one goal in every classroom is for kids to care for each other. Build a community of compassion, caring, and friendship. Take an honest look in the mirror at the policies and procedures used. Are they divisive? Are students compared to each other? Is one student publicly complimented with the implication others are not doing as well? Are some left out of activities, games and field trips, while others go? Do students choose friends to eat lunch with the teacher or spend extra time on the playground? It is our responsibility to create an environment that promotes peace, respect, and friendship.

CHAPTER 8

~

Rewards and Bribes: What is the Difference?

For the most part, I believe rewards are good and if used correctly help teach responsibility. For the most part I believe bribes are not good because they teach kids to be deceptive and sneaky. Bribing often leads to entitlement. The way to tell the difference between the two is that rewards happen after a behavior and bribes before. "If you behave all week there will be Fun Friday," is a bribe because behaving has not happened yet. "Because you behaved all week I am deciding to give Fun Friday" is a reward because behaving hasn't happened yet.

Reward Everyone in Honor of One: I touched on this last chapter. Reward the entire class, school, or team in honor of a student or group of students. This builds culture, climate and community. It is also a way to include a student who chronically misbehaves. Minutes before "Fun Friday" or the field trip, tell the student who was not going to be allowed to participate that he is now allowed. To that individual, privately say, "I am still not happy with you, but because of Erica everyone gets to go and you are part of everyone. Please thank Erica, not me because I am still not happy with you!" Occasionally I pick two students that are arguing or upset with each other and set a scenario so one is rewarded in honor of the other. Almost never punish everyone because of one as this often leads to anger, frustration and annoyance.

If I Want to Give a Student Something Extra: Do it privately. Try avoiding public announcements and making a scene. For example, "Because Erica behaved this week everyone gets 15 extra minutes on the playground in honor of her. Do not thank me, thank her." When everyone is on the playground pull Erica aside privately and say: "By the way, here is a free homework pass. I will not discuss this with anyone else. Thanks for being so awesome this week." Then walk away.

Are Students Ever Left Out? Occasionally a student is kept out of recess or excluded from a field trip if safety is an issue. Just be sure to weigh long-term effects of this. Will excluding teach the student to improve behavior? Is the potential of building more resentment, hostility, and anger worth it? Sometimes the answer is yes because the student needs to understand certain privileges must be earned. This is why it is so important not to predetermine consequences or threaten certain actions unless you can be sure that you will be able to follow through.

My Sticker and Ticket Detox Program: Sometimes people ask what I think of stickers and tickets. If given privately or to all in honor of one or two I am fine. It is frustrating when kids say, "Last year we got stickers when we did that. Why aren't we getting them this year? How many tickets did I earn by doing the right thing?" When teaching fourth grade I decided to detoxify them. At the first opportunity I say in a soft and calm voice, "Did someone say they want a ticket or sticker? I will pretend not to hear that. Obviously nobody told you stickers and tickets are not cool anymore. They are for little kids like third graders. Many of you are ten years old, which means double digits. Double digits means it is not ok to say out loud you like stickers anymore." Usually a student in back shouts, "Yea stickers are dumb" and now you've got them. For those whose world you just destroyed tell them not to worry you are still giving tickets and stickers. From now on they are given privately and charts always kept at home or in a private place. If teaching third grade I say they are for little kids like second graders, and so on. In kindergarten I never have to give cigarettes, I mean stickers, in the first place.

Concluding Thought: Bribing definitely gains better / improved behavior in the presence of authority, but this should not be good enough. Adults are not walking or riding home on the bus from school. They are not in locker rooms or sitting at the lunch table. The goal is for kids to do the right thing because it is the right thing, not because they get things for it. I believe administrators should do the same. My former principal frequently began staff meetings by praising us as a whole. "Thank you so much for the extra work all of you put in." Then she glanced at certain people saying, "I know many of you are staying after to help struggling learners. Thank you. I saw others pick up garbage in the hall you did not drop. The band concert was excellent. Thanks to everyone for such a great job. As a faculty you are amazing." That's it. Stickers or tickets are not handed out to spend at a teacher store. One time we walked into a room filled with food. She said, "Congratulations to Miss Levy. She was selected teacher of the year by our district and could not have done it without all of you. The food is for everyone in honor of her. Thanks for all you do." This is how to build culture among staff.

CHAPTER 9

~

Group Work and Transition

The effectiveness of many instructional moments depends upon how well students work together. This is especially true during cooperative learning (group) activities. When groups are well organized, there is often no better form of learning. When disorganized they are a chaotic nightmare ripe for disruption. Here are my cooperative learning and transition essentials:

- **No More than Five Members:** Six or more will flirt with disaster.

- **Each Group Member has a Specific Role:** Number each member one through five and ask them not to forget their number. Each number correlates with a task. No matter the activity, grade level, or content area, number ones and fives never change for me. They are always the same. All other roles will change depending on the activity. I say, "Number one in each group is the leader. Your only job is to make sure everyone else does his or her job. Number two is reader. Your job is to read the short story to the group. Number three takes notes. Number four is note organizer so number five can present the most important points to the class. Number five is speaker / presenter. Number five can't do her job without organized notes. Number four can't organize notes if number three does not take them. Number three can't take them if number two reads fast. Number one makes sure this whole thing works so I don't have to."

- **Only Talk to Leaders:** Say, "During group time there are six people allowed to talk to Mr. Mendler. If you are not a group leader and have a question ask your group leader first. If they can't help they come to me." I am the CEO of the classroom. My name is on the door. Group leader one is director of sales and marketing. Leader two is in charge of Human Resources. Regular sales people do not report right to the CEO. Go to your manager. They come to me. Instead of managing 30, I focus on six. They manage everyone else for me. This is classroom management. Classroom management is getting kids to work for instead of against you. It is teaching leadership. If anyone is upset explain this is what referees do to manage a field. Before the game starts they call captains to the center. "Number seven and nine are captains. They talk to the referee. Everyone else goes to them." Instead of managing 22 players on a football field they manage four.

- **Red Cup, Yellow Cup, Green Cup:** Next I gather leaders around me like I am coaching a basketball team. Each is given one red, one yellow, and one green plastic drinking cup. Green in front means everything is good. We are on track to get it done. Yellow in front tells me quick question. How long do we have again for this? How do you pronounce this word? Questions that allow me to slow down to answer without stopping. Red tells me you are stuck and need extra help.

- **Rig the Groups:** Some kids need extra direct instruction from their teacher. Occasionally put your lowest kids together. Act like they are doing the same group work as everyone else. When everyone else starts working sit with the lowest (or highest) group and say, "Ok the five of you and me are working on multiplication for the next 15 minutes. Here we go."

- **Do Kids get Different Roles Every day?** Not necessarily. I put people where they are best when their actions directly affect four others. The Yankees do not put their starting shortstop at catcher just to change it up. Some kids are natural leaders. Others are better at reading or organizing. This is not the time to teach a student how to read. The group leader gets a lot of power to make decisions during the activity. Sort of like I am the general manager in the press box and the group leader manages on the field. The only position they cannot touch is speaker / presenter. Besides that, the leader can move people if they see fit.

- **Tell the Two T's:** Once groups are settled the first "T" is time. Tell how long the activity should take then ask students to repeat. "We only have seven minutes for this activity. How many minutes?" After they repeat tell the second "T" which is task. Explain exactly what they will do.

- **It is Easier to Extend Than Take Away:** I like to figure out how much time the activity will take and then cut it in half. The goal is to create a sense of urgency. If it should take 20 minutes I say, "Let's go everyone. You only have ten minutes to complete this." Urgency usually leads to action. I want them getting right to work. If the ten-minute mark comes and groups are working well it is easy to extend. By contrast, try taking time away, and someone always complains.

- **Energy Matters:** I recently worked in an elementary school outside Albany, NY. The first teacher has 26 students in her class. Kids sit on the rug and listen to a story. When the teacher finishes she says, "Ok everyone back to your seats." They start wandering. She pleads, "C'mon guys! Back to your seats now. You guys!" The next teacher has 31 in her class. She too reads a story. With one page left she stops reading and looks at her kids. "The second I finish this page we head back to our seats. We do not get a drink or go to the bathroom. We do not ask any questions. We go heading right back to our seats. Where do we go?" They reply, "Back to our seats." In the most calming voice she finishes the story, stands up, and says, "Lets go! Lets go! Lets go! Back to your seats now! You are not moving fast enough. Hurry. Hurry. Hurry." She has more energy during the transition than during the story.

- **Teach Through the Transition:** Youtube has mastered the art of transition. Recently I was watching an old episode of Seinfeld. The episode ends and before I can shut it off another begins. It used to be a show ended, credits rolled, commercials followed, and next show began. Not anymore. Youtube realizes once they lose a viewer, it is hard to get them back. Transitioning from one subject or activity to another can be a source of disruption in school. Tip number one is teach through the transition. Do not stop. For example, I often hear, "We are finished with writing. Take a five minute break and start Science." Instead say, "You have one minute to return to your seat for Science. While returning watch the demonstration I do. Walk, look and listen at the same time." In workshops I do an activity where people work with partners, usually someone on the opposite side of the room. When the activity finishes I instruct them back by saying, "As you head back I am sharing the most important strategy of the day." A few minutes into the new activity individual kids can take breaks if needed.

Concluding Thought: Groups work best when each student has a clearly defined role. Let them know only leaders talk to the teacher. If any other member is struggling they go to the group leader first. Occasionally I allow kids to pick partners. Just be aware and prepared for most picking friends and the same few frequently left out.

CHAPTER 10

~

Defuse Power Struggles

Power Struggles usually happen for one reason. Both unwilling to budge, the student and teacher both do not want to look bad in front of the class. This shows the importance of privacy. The following example happened recently in a class I observed.

Teacher: "Jasmine, pick that piece of paper up young lady. We don't drop papers on the floor and leave them there."

Jasmine: "I didn't drop it."

Teacher: "I saw you. You have five seconds to pick it up. Five, four, three..."

Jasmine: "I didn't drop it and I'm not picking it up. Keep counting."

Teacher: "You can move your clip then go to the office."

Jasmine: "You can't make me."

Teacher: "I'll call the office and they will come get you."

Jasmine: "You think I care? Go ahead, b*tch."

Teacher: "What did you call me?"

Jasmine: "You heard me."

Teacher: "That's it. You're gone."

If lucky, Jasmine slams the door open and leaves. Not lucky means she stays. The worst I ever saw was in Savannah GA. A kindergarten teacher tries kicking a kindergartner out. She says, "Leave now!" He says, "Nah I am good." She reaches for him and he starts running around the room. Ever see a six-year-old run around the room? They are fast. Kids rarely go straight to the office when storming out of class. They go to the gym and the lunchroom. Sometimes they even come back and wave at us. Many meet with other kids kicked out of their classes. Some form their own cooperative learning groups. Eventually they get to the office. By the time this happens most are completely calm. Regulars go right for their chair. Some are actually annoyed if someone is in their seat. People often ask me why difficult kids and administrative secretaries are such good friends. They are the two loneliest groups of people in a school.

Secretary: "You again?"

Me: "Yea. But it wasn't my fault. Admit you don't like her either! Your kids go here and they don't have her." By the end most offer me coffee. I am going to pick on everyone now, meaning nobody is allowed to get offended. Starting with administrators.

Admin: "What did you do?"

Kid: "Nothing."

Admin: "Why are you here?"

Kid: "I have no idea. Maybe I called her a b*tch, but she is one. You ever see how she talks to kids? That lady is so rude and my brother had her last year and said the same thing about her then. My mom had her like 25 years ago. Can't you find anybody younger?"

I feel bad for administrators because they usually hear the kid's side of the story first. The kids are good. They tell stories. Then the teacher side comes in on a well-written (eye roll) referral form. If you still hand write them you can feel the ink on the paper. The pen pierces four carbon copies always saying the same thing: Disrespectful. Rude. Uncooperative. I am waiting for a teacher to write the truth on a referral form. "Someone had to leave and the contract says it cannot be me so I sent you her. I will take a three day suspension please, with pay." I am joking. Part of my job here is to entertain you, but in school this is serious business. Rewind to Jasmine not picking up the paper. She is suspended two days for disrespect and insubordination because a piece of paper is on the floor and a teacher is unable/willing to defuse. Sadly, this is not uncommon in many classrooms. Minor disagreements turn to massive explosions. Fortunately, this can be defused with a different approach. I have two goals when a power struggle is forming. First, keep the student in class. Second, get back to teaching. I am not trying to save face. I am not trying to win an argument. I am not trying to teach about the real world. I am trying to keep the student here and get back to teaching. Nothing else. With this in mind, next time a battle forms, unleash my world famous Five W's of Defusing. I've written a lot about how important it is to be private. However, in the situation with Jasmine things are not private anymore. The first "W" is simple. In the loudest deepest tone you can muster unleash the word "WHOA!" The goal is for all kids to instinctively look at you. The second they do (and second "W") tell the student WHAT is happening. "Whoa! You and I are about to argue right now." Notice I don't say it is her fault. I don't say she is rude. I don't say she is disruptive. I don't say she is inappropriate. You and I both together are about to argue. Then I tell WHY it is happening. "Whoa! You and I are about to argue right now. You don't want to look bad in front of your friends and I don't want to look bad in front of the class." Next comes WHEN to deal with it because you can't leave upset kids hanging. "Whoa! You and I are about to argue right now. You don't want to look bad in front of your friends and I don't either. I promise the second class is over we will finish this discussion. Thank you so much for waiting until then. I know you are upset but thanks for waiting until then." Then WALK away both physically and mentally. The student will mumble, you get the second to last word, power struggle defused. Again, the process is:

Whoa: Tone private as possible but loud enough to leave no doubt. The goal is to startle. Unfortunately, the whole class might look. Eye contact is with the ceiling.

What: Tone quieter but still passionate, moving closer to student. Lower to his level or slightly above but stay out of reach. Make direct and firm eye contact (unless you feel this is overly threatening to the student): "You and I are about to argue right now."

Why: Tone even quieter. Still make direct and firm eye contact. Get even closer and maintain his level or slightly above. Be sure not to spit or have horrible breath. "You don't want to look bad in front of your friends, nor do I."

When: Tone even quieter. Hand almost completely covers teacher mouth. Hold eye contact through the words "Thank you." Move quickly to walk away, but slow down when getting behind him. Lean as close to back of student head as possible looking away and whisper, "for waiting until after class." It is important not to whisper directly in the ear. Make sure they know you are there but always whisper to the back of the head. Expect a mumble or two. Remember second to last word.

Walk: Walk away with intent and purpose. If he continues to mumble repeat, "Thanks for waiting until after class. I appreciate it so much." You are modeling how to walk away from an argument. You are going to use this as a teachable moment later. Continue to move.

Use Humor: I am not asking you to become a clown or jokester. That said, tense situations are easily defused by humor and often leave kids speechless. I am reminded of an eighth grader who told my co-teacher to go f*ck herself. Her response; "I will be doing that later but it is none of your business." (mic drop walk away). My former student Brittany one day unprovoked called me a, "Giraffe looking mother f*ck*r" to my face. I was in a strange mood that day and asked the class, "Do I look like a giraffe?" To which one replied, "Actually you have a long neck and a big nose, Mr. Mendler. You kind of do." My response, "Brittany, great job on your animal choice to describe me. Looks like everyone agrees." One of my favorite humor stories happened in Texas. A sixth grade boy said to his teacher, "I ain't takin' out my books you AIDS having hoe. Her response, "It is exactly for that reason I am not in a very good mood

66

today. So take out your books and let's go. Now!"

Use L.A.A.D.

Listen: Hear what the student says, not how he says it.
Acknowledge: Let the student know you hear him.
Agree: Let the student know he is or might be right.
Defer: Let the student know when you are available to finish the conversation.

Is Removal Ever an Option? Yes. My first year teaching I kicked kids out for everything. One day my former principal slams the door open to my room. She says, "What are you doing?" I tell her, "Teaching. Everything is going great." She says, "I am sure it is. 12 of your kids are in my office." I had eight left and it was going great. She says, "I will be back" and walks out. Later she comes back.

Her: "Here is the deal, Brian. For the rest of the year you are never allowed to send me another kid. I don't pay you to teach nice kids. I don't pay you to teach friendly kids, and I don't pay you to teach kids who like English class. I pay you to get kids who hate reading on the first day to love it by the last. Nothing more. Stop whining, stop complaining and start teaching. Do you understand me?"

Me: (knees knocking) "Yes."

Her: "Mr. Decamp is waiting for you. He never has a problem with the same kids you always have a problem with. If he never has a problem and you always have a problem, who do you think the problem is?"

Me: "Me?"

Her: "I knew you were smart."

My conversation with Mr. Decamp:

Mr. D: "I am willing to work with you under one condition. No matter what I say you are not allowed to get defensive."

Me: "No problem."

Mr. D: "Your problem is you don't give a sh*t about the kids."

Me: "Yes I do."

Mr. D: "I am done."

Me: "Wait. I feel like I care. I want to care. What do you mean?"

Mr. D: "Tell me about Angel Cruz's home life."

Me: "Angel Cruz. It is bad. I mean I know it is not good. He has lots of brothers and sisters. I think maybe like five. His mom, or wait maybe it is his grandma, actually I am not sure who it is but I know she is nice. I am pretty sure that…"

Mr. D: "Stop you are making me sick. Ask me about Angel's home life so I can show you what it sounds like when you actually know a kid."

Me: "Can you please tell me about Angel Cruz's home life?"

Mr. D: "It is not good. He is the youngest of seven kids, three brothers and three sisters. Some days he literally fights for food at home. His mother is one of the nicest people you will meet. Problem is she works two full time jobs. At the courthouse from nine to five, home for an hour, then seven to midnight at UPS moving packages off a conveyor belt. His father walked out on the family two years ago this week. This matters because he does not trust adults, and he really does not trust adult men. You don't know anything about these kids. Get out of here and go do your job." From that moment on it became people over product and kids over content, always. I managed not to kick anyone out the rest of that year. The first day of my second year my principal comes back to my room. She says, "Now you are allowed to remove kids." I say, "I don't need to anymore." She says, "That's why you are allowed." Then she explains two times it is okay to: "Throw away a young person's education to save 24 others." She draws home plate and two batters boxes on my whiteboard. In box one she writes, "Literally so bad you cannot teach." In box two she writes, "Physical Violence." Then she says, "We have a rule at this school saying kids can't wear hats. A student is wearing a hat. This is not ground for removal because it does not fit one of the two categories. From now on any time anything happens immediately, see if it fits a box. If not 100% of your energy focuses on handling in class."

How to Remove a Student:

Mr. M: (always privately if possible, at or a notch below student level) "Your behavior is so rude and inappropriate I can't teach anymore. If you need to go, feel free. I prefer you stay and behave because you are important and I will miss you when gone. Please come back when ready to learn. I hope that is very soon but go if you need to." Then walk away. First I set a limit. "Your behavior is so rude and inappropriate I can't teach." Second I tell the student my "truth sandwich." The first and last statements (two pieces of bread) are true. The middle two statements (meat) might not be true, but I say them anyway to protect myself later. Truth one (bread): "I prefer you stay and behave." I always prefer this. False one and two (meat): "Because you are important to our class (probably not) and I will miss you when gone (probably I won't)." Truth two (bread): "Come back when ready to learn." His parent calls, "Why you kicking my kid out of class?" Now I say, "Not only did I not kick him out, I told him I prefer he stay and behave, he is important, I will miss him when gone, and to come back when ready to learn. Want to know how it got this far because it takes a lot to get me upset." Notice I do not kick her out. I offer the door. 50% of the time she will leave. 50% of the time she stays. If she leaves there are two options. Option one only works with another adult in the room. Count back from ten to one. Turn the class over to your aid, co-teacher, student teacher, or administrator and go find her. The conversation sounds like this:

Me: "I am sorry."

Her: "I hate you. This class sucks. You are stupid. Get away from me!"

Me: "I know and I said I am sorry."

Step one in the process is to calm the person down. Say, "I am sorry" over and over until relatively calm. Keep distance and make eye contact. My record with a kid is 27. Once calm, my job is to become her teammate. I want her to see we are similar. It is hard to coach a kid if she does not believe we are teammates first.

Me: "Have you ever made a mistake in your life?"

Her: "Well, yeah."

Me: "When you say 'sorry' do you want people to forgive you?"

Her: "Yeah."

Me: "I am just like you. Sometimes I am impulsive and say things I don't mean. Kind of like you. Sometimes I am rude, nasty, and inappropriate, just like someone else we know. It is scary how similar we are." Step three in the process is to coach. Coaching means I show a new way to hold a baseball bat. I show a new way to complete a multiplication problem. I show a new way to hold a guitar. I show a new way to handle anger.

Me: "A good rule to remember in life is, 'If it feels really good in the short term it is probably really bad in the long term.' Punching someone feels really good in the short term. No question it does. After the punch you get in trouble. Your parents get called. You get suspended. You miss more school. You get farther behind. You have to attend summer school. Long term, you hurt you."

Me: "Why do you want to hurt yourself?"

Her: "I don't."

Me: "Of course not. Want to learn how I handle anger when I feel like punching someone?"

Her: "Yea."

Me: "Close your eyes. Picture someone you wouldn't mind punching. On the count of three punch her hard but use your breath instead of hands. One, two, three." She will probably take a very short breath. Tell her, "No. This time you count and I show what it sounds like to knock someone out with breath."

Her: "One, two, three." I inhale as long as possible and exhale so loud I wake up all sleeping students two hallways over. She practices until this becomes her response every time. Counselors often tell kids to take deep breaths when angry. This is not enough for kids who feel like knocking someone out. Truth is she does take a deep breath but I phrase it very

70

differently. Bottom line is this conversation must happen or she will continue to behave the same way. The other 50% of the time she will stay. Half of that time she will stay and behave. This means "offering the door" keeps the student in class and behaving 25% of the overall time. This is great for the toughest kids.

Challenge Oppositional Kids: My number one motivator in life is when people tell me I cannot accomplish something. Energy and excitement overtake my body and I feel an overwhelming desire to prove them wrong. Maybe it comes from feeling inadequate as a child. Maybe it comes from feeling like people never truly believed in me when I was a kid. I don't know where it comes from. I do know I love it. Most people enjoy being challenged if the challenge can be successfully accomplished. If, however, the ability to succeed is impossible challenge leads to annoyance, frustration, and resentment. Challenging a blind person to read the board will overwhelm them every time. The following example challenges students to behave for a substitute when I am gone.

Mr. M: "I will not be here tomorrow because I am attending a workshop. The expectation is for you to behave when I am gone. I look forward to a great report when I get back." Most teachers bribe and / or threaten next. "If you are good while I am gone you will get…" Or, "If you do not behave while I am gone this will happen to you." Instead, I dismiss the class. As they are leaving, pull the leaders aside. Privately say, "Did you hear what I said to the class about behaving tomorrow when I am gone? I lied. I don't care how they behave. There are two names I am looking for when I return. We know you can influence everyone to misbehave while I am gone. We've seen it a bunch of times. I don't think you have it in you to get them to behave. I guess we will see won't we? I look forward to reading the report when I return." Then walk away. Many students will do the right thing to prove you wrong. When it happens, do not act excited and shower him with praise. Instead say, "So you are well behaved for one lousy day while I am gone. I don't think you

71

can behave for a whole week while I am here." Again walk away both physically and mentally.

Concluding Thought: Power struggles almost never happen in private. Apologize to students, even when feeling you did nothing wrong. My favorite line is, "I am sorry someone in our class got that upset. This is never my intention." Use the five W's to defuse. Thank students before they complete a task. Please stop complaining and stop saying, "I don't feel like I am supported." The job of a boss is not always to support the employee. The boss is there to make us better. This means telling the truth. When I do a good job, tell me. When I don't, tell me. Everyone please stop getting offended.

EPILOGUE

~

Teacher that Changed my Life

I am in sixth grade gym class shooting baskets. My principal enters and says to me, "Mr. Dalton wants to see you." Mr. Dalton is an older man with white spikey hair. He wears fat bow ties and cardigan sweaters with khaki slacks and brown shoes, every day. This day he sits at his desk, feet up, reading the New York Times. Without looking he shouts, "Sit down." It startles me. My instinct is to argue, but I don't because there is no one else in the room. The audience plays a role in every performance. He slides his chair next to me and stares with a crazy look in his eyes. It feels like eternity but only lasts a minute or so. Then he points his finger at me. He never makes contact but he gets close.

Mr. Dalton: "I want to tell you something right now that I don't ever want you to forget."

Me: "Yeah, what?"

Mr. Dalton: "I want to tell you how much I love having you in my class. I love it."

Me: "Yeah well you can, you are, you should. Wait, what did you say?"

Mr. Dalton: (pointing to his face) "I love it. You see this face? Get used to it. You are my favorite kind of kid." I do not realize at the time kids are like ice cream flavors. There are different kinds of kids. You ever think to yourself, "If I could put this kid's brain in this kid's body I'd have the ideal kid." You can't, yet. This was so different from anything I was

73

used to hearing. We sit in silence for a few seconds then he asks me a question.

Mr. Dalton: "Who you are is really good. I really like who you are. I believe I can help you get better at being who you already are. Would you like that?" Finally, someone tells me I don't have to be more like my brother or the kid who sits perfectly still. You mean I can just be me and that will be good enough for someone? I put two words together in that moment I never said to a teacher before, "Yes please." Please someone help me. Please someone stop consequencing me. Please stop kicking me out. Please stop making me someone else's problem and start working with me! Isn't that your job? When I was a ten-year-old kid I did not know how to say it, but I know how to say so today and I will not stop. For every kid in your school who comes every day and nobody says, "I know we argue. I know we battle. I know we fight. The truth is you drive me utterly crazy, but I would not have it any other way. I love working with kids like you." This means so much more than a ticket or sticker. Why not make this your behavior program? Every teacher is required to say to their most challenging student, "I love having you in my class. You make me a better teacher and for that I am grateful." I don't understand why this is so hard for so many.

Mr. Dalton: "Good we start tomorrow."

Me: "Start what?"

Mr. Dalton: "I know kids like you. You love being the center of attention. You love having everyone look at you. You love being in the middle of all the action all the time (I still love it). It's good."

Me: "It's good?"

Mr. Dalton: "It's good. You ever see Leno or Letterman or Seinfeld or Chris Rock? They have hundreds of jokes but only tell the four or five best. After that no one listens anymore. You need to learn how to shut it off so when on you are a lot more effective."

Me: "I don't know how to shut it off." Severe ADHD does not come with an off switch.

Mr. Dalton: "Tomorrow in class you get five minutes or three jokes."

Me: "You are going to let me tell jokes in class?"

Mr. Dalton: "Yes."

Me: "I never met a teacher who likes jokes."

Mr. Dalton: (with a hint of sarcasm) "We all like jokes. We just don't like hundreds of them. You can count to three, right?" I believe sarcasm is like a dangerous chemical in the chemistry lab. Used incorrectly it blows up relationships. Used properly it creates cool bubbling demonstrations that hook kids. I have two rules for using sarcasm.

1. **If the Student does not get it, Apologize Fast.**

   Kid: "Why you saying that to me?"

   Me: "I am totally joking. I am so sorry. I really am sorry."

   Kid: "You don't know me good enough to joke."

   Me: "Ok and I said sorry. Have you ever made a mistake in your life? When you say sorry don't you want people to forgive you? I am just like you. I make mistakes too and I made one. I am sorry."

2. **If you are Going to Dish it you Have to Take it.** There is not much worse than a teacher messing with a kid. The kid messes back and the teacher writes a referral. Either dish it and take it or do neither. Sometimes kids will get you good. Remember Dan from earlier? I recall a day he had a bright neon yellow polo shirt on.

   Me: "Hey I love that shirt. It looks good on you. You know it would look better on me though, right?"

   Dan: "Why would it look better on you?"

   Me: "Because I am better looking than you."

   Dan: "You know what I have on that will look really good on you for real?"

   Me: "What?"

   Dan: "Hair, son."

Then Mr. Dalton says his other famous line. He had two of them. "Sit

75

down" and "Get out of here." I get almost to the door but he stops me:

Mr. Dalton: "Brian, real quick."

Me: "What?"

Mr. Dalton: "Want this to be like real life?"

Me: "I don't know what do you mean?"

Mr. Dalton: "What I mean is, if you stink we can boo. We can boo you right off the stage. Like in a real comedy club."

Me: "Yea."

Mr. Dalton: "Cool. See ya."

I get home that night and my mom is there. I say, "Mom, I have this English teacher Mr. Dalton who is letting me tell jokes in class." She does not buy a word of it. I say, "Really mom, call him." She does.

Mom: "Hi Mr. Dalton it's Mrs. Mendler."

Mr. Dalton: "Hey Mrs. Mendler I am not sure why you are calling but before you say anything I want to tell you about your son. Number one he is smart. Number two he is a leader. Yes he will tell jokes! Your son is funny. He holds people's attention better than most adults I know. Only three jokes though because after that nobody is really listening anymore. He can count to three, right?"

Mom: "I think."

Before this phone call there were dozens of others from many other teachers all ending with my mother crying or yelling. Not this one. This one she has that "proud of" look in her eye. I remember thinking, "Why don't all the teachers do this? Someday if I am a teacher I will do the opposite of what they all do. Instead of calling home to metaphorically kick the kid in the head a few more times, I will do the opposite. I will call to say how amazing he is. I would have run through a brick wall for Mr. Dalton in that moment. The next day I get to school and for the first time I feel really good about being there. For the first time a teacher values what I am good at. Not what I am supposed to be good at, but what I am good at. I tell two jokes that day and they did not boo. In fact they haven't booed yet and I haven't sat down. My sixth grade teacher got me started in what I do today. For that I will always be grateful. I start the third joke but a few words in realize it is not very good and still needs work. I look at Mr. Dalton (sitting in my seat, right in front).

Me: "That's it I am done." All of a sudden the crazy look comes back in his eyes. He jumps out of the chair landing inches from my face, his back facing the class.

Mr. Dalton: "Don't you dare ever do this to me again!"

Me: "What did I do? They didn't boo."

Mr. Dalton: "I told you five minutes and three jokes. You only did three minutes and two jokes. Now I have to teach longer, sh*t!"

You have no idea how that man had my heart racing. Twenty something years later I think about how overwhelmingly blessed I am in life. To the point I would not change one thing because I believe in life what you go through leads you. I hope and pray that someday there will be a kid who was kicked out of school, struggles with reading, and in addiction recovery. You won't believe what they will be doing with their life. Flying in airplanes, staying in hotels and traveling all over the world telling their story. When finished and everyone is exhausted and does not want to read anymore they are going to say, "I know but you have to hear about this one teacher. His name is Mr. Mendler and he is relentless. When everyone quit on me he didn't. When everyone said they didn't want me in their class he took me. Because of him, I am here today--because of him." Now it is your turn. I can't do it for you, but I can lead you there. Each of you has to decide the impact you will have on these kids for the rest of your career. Every time I work with adults I talk about two of them that dramatically impacted my life. I talk about Mrs. Mills who I believe came to work every day to make kids miserable. I talk about Mr. Dalton who did the opposite. I do not believe there is an in between. Everyone in between is forgotten and I promise I won't be forgotten. I'd rather be Mrs. Mills than be forgotten. At least people remember that lady for something. The last promise I will make is that your challenging students probably will not thank you for reading this book. On behalf of them, I will thank you. Thank you so much for all you do for kids, and I wish you best of luck in the future.

RECOMMENDED RESOURCES

~

Starfall.com	1st grade mathematics and reading
Mysterydoug.com	5-minute educational videos
Noredink.com	Build better writers
ClassDojo.com	Classroom communication app
IXL.com	Comprehensive K-12 curriculum
Scratch.mit.edu	Create stories, games and animations
Mobymax.com	Fix K-8 learning gaps
Watchknowlearn.org	Free K-12 educational videos
Google classroom	Free web service for schools/non-profits
Kahoot.it	Game-based learning and trivia platform
Raz-kids.com	Guided reading
Mathequalslove.blogspot.com	High School Math and Physical Science
Prekinders.com	Ideas and resources for Pre-K and Preschool
Code.org	K-12 computer science
Imaginelearning.com	K-12 digital language, literacy and math
Tolerance.org	K-12 program emphasizing social justice and anti-bias
Wonderopolis.org	K-12; Exploring wonders of learning
PebbleGo.com	K-2 readers
Interactivesites.weebly.com	K-5 online, interactive and educational games
Channelone.com	Kids News
Achieve3000.com	Literacy
Flocabulary.com	Literacy
prodigygame.com	Math 1st-8th
LearningFarm.com	Math and Reading; K-8
Reflexmath.com	Math for grades 2+
Zearn.org	Math K-5
Dreambox.com	Math PreK-8
freckle.com	Math, ELA, Social Studies and Science
sumdog.com	Math, spelling, reading

Theartofed.com	Online resource for art teachers
teachyourmonstertoread.com	Phonics and reading
Myon.com	Reading
Newsela.com	Reading
Readwritethink.org	Reading and Language Arts
Readtheory.org	Reading and writing
Readworks.org	Reading comprehension K-12
Commonlit.org	Reading passages in literary and nonfiction genres for 3rd-12th
Nearpod.com	Ready-to-teach K-12 lessons
sciencebuddies.org	Science
Quizizz.com	Self-paced quizzes
Flipgrid.com	Social and emotional learning

SPECIAL THANKS

~

Laurie Abbazia	Teacher	Rochester, NY
Morningstar Academy	Teachers and Staff	Brunswick, GA
Sara Ann Alexander	Secondary ELA Teacher	Bowling Green, KY
Kelly Alexander	Family Advocate/Social Worker	Cleveland, OH
Stephanie Allen	Grade 3 Teacher	Pulaski, NY
Kim Alowitz	ESOL Teacher	West Des Moines, IA
Heidi Anderson	2nd Grade Teacher	Princeton, IL
Gregory Annoni	Assistant Principal	Macungie, PA
Sandy Austin	Retired Teacher	Indianapolis, IN
Deirdre Bachar	Title One Reading	Fairfield, IA
Selime Baftiri Ballazhi	World Language Teacher HS	Tinley Park, IL
Michelle Bahnsen	Behavior Coach	Des Moines, IA
Brenda Baker	Special Education Teacher	Cambridge Springs, PA
Sarah Baker	Assistant Principal	Bowling Green, KY
Brooke Balderson	Literacy Coach	Annapolis, MD
Kerri Ball	First Grade Teacher	Ola, AR
Nora Ballwanz	SPED Teacher	Fond du Lac, WI
Codi Battaglia	2nd Grade Teacher	Rochester, NY
Thomas J. Bauer	Investigator – Juvenile Officer	River Falls, WI
Kim Bauer	Educator (5th grade science/social studies)	Pickerington, OH
Karleen Bender	Special Education Teacher	Boone, IA
Lana Beres	Instructional Strategist	Des Moines, IA
Stephanie Berry Dunson	4th Grade	Brunswick, GA
Stacey Bex	School Psychologist	Terre Haute, IN
Jennifer Blake	Principal	California City, CA
Aimee Blomster	Paraprofessional	North Branford, CT
Carolyn Blount	Special Education Teacher	Pulaski, NY
Dr. Candice Boatright	Principal	Union County, NC
Jessica Boe	Associate Principal	Joliet, IL
Peter D. Boland	English Teacher	Woonsocket, RI
Theresa Boniface	1st Grade Teacher	Niagara Falls, NY
Michelle Boyd	Title One Specialist	Bluefield, WV

Janet Boyd	Aide	Columbus, OH
Tiffany Bradford ED.S	Special Education Teacher	Hattiesburg, MS
Krystal Brandt	Music Specialist	Sugar Land, TX
Katie Braun	Intervention Specialist	Mentor, OH
Heather Briggs	Second Grade Teacher	Ames, IA
Lauren Brothers	First Grade Teacher	Douglas, AL
Sara Brown	Elementary Special Education	Des Moines, IA
Nicole Bullington	Special Education Director	Iroquois County, IL
Julia Buman	Teacher DMPS Home Instruction	Des Moines, IA
Mary Burgess	4th Grade	Albany, NY
Jill Burke	K-5 School Leader	Des Moines, IA
Sheryl Burkhart	Assistant Principal	Flandreau, SD
Ann Busby	Academic Manager	Ocala, FL
Erik D. Bushey	Student Support Coordinator	Alburgh, VT
Katie Butcher	4th Grade Teacher	Denver, CO
Brianne Butler	Kindergarten/RTI Teacher	Mt. Healthy, OH
Alejandra Cantu	Special Education Teacher	Mission, TX
Adriane Carlson	At-Risk Student Supports Coordinator	Waterloo, IA
Emma Casas-Valadez	Teacher	Pleasanton, TX
Taylor Caven	Orchestra Director	Bowling Green, KY
Sarah Chapman	Intervention Specialist	Kent, OH
Jessica Cline	ESL Teacher	Bowling Green, KY
Marissa Cokeley	Special Education Teacher	Des Moines, IA
Jessica Cole	Life Skills Special Ed Teacher	Joliet, IL
Lynsey Comer	Intervention	Pickerington, OH
Sarah Coniglio	Special Education	Mount Morris, NY
Sarah Cooper	School Counselor	West Des Moines, IA
Heather Cope	Intervention Specialist	Cincinnati, OH
Diane Corley	Assistant Principal	Phoenix, AZ
Jared Coughlan	Teacher	West Sacramento, CA
Tarina Cox-Jones	Principal	Omaha, NE
Lisa Crawford	Teacher	Grand Rapids, MI
Amanda Criddle	Kindergarten Teacher	Lockport, NY
Susan Crimmins	Preschool Teacher	Des Moines, IA
Crystal Crowdis	Head Start Teacher	Des Moines, IA
Kim Crumbley	1st Grade Teacher	Brunswick, GA
Stacie Cummings	Adapted PE and Health Teacher	Ashville, NY
Karen Currie	Elementary Social Worker	Southfield, MI
Theresa Curry	Health Lab Teacher	Joliet, IL
Kristi Curtis	1st Grade Teacher	Des Moines, IA
Lindzy Curtis	2nd Grade Teacher	Wanatah, IN
Suzanne Davis	Special Education Consultant	Bowling Green, KY

Michele DeBruler	Principal	Luling, LA
Sara Deel	ELA Teacher	Bowling Green, KY
Ondrea Dellmann	Third Grade	Ames, IA
Dawn Dickinson	Health Teacher	Joliet, IL
Cheryl Disrud	Title 1/1-7th Computer	St. John, ND
Lisa Dobson	SPED Associate	Des Moines, IA
Jennifer Dugas	ED Teacher	Luling, LA
April Edgy Kelly	School Counselor	Brunswick, GA
Amber Emerson	Science Teacher	Tuscaloosa, AL
Laura Espinoza	Technology Integration Teacher	Perth, Australia
Joe Evenden	CATE Teacher	Beaufort, SC
Donna Faller	8:1:1 Special Education Teacher	Allegany, NY
Bethanne Falther	5th Grade Math/Science Teacher	Pickerington, OH
Michele Farley	Instructional Coach	Ontario Center, NY
Alii Farrell	ELA/SPED High School Teacher	Fairport, NY
Laura Fead	Assistant Principal	Las Vegas, NV
Cindy Felkins	Special Education Director	Cochran, GA
Kristin Floyd	3rd Grade Teacher	Ashtabula, OH
Sherman Flucas II	C.V.O./Founder of LegacyMindset	Indianapolis, IN
Bridget Foes	Special Needs Coordinator and Teacher	Princeton, IL
Casey Force	Special Education Consultant	Des Moines, IA
Jane Ford	Kindergarten	Lockport, NY
Jessica Fuselier-Rhodes	Teacher	Danbury, TX
Shelly Gagliardi	Special Education Teacher	Cannelton, IN
Kathleen Garland	Principal/CEO	Pittsburgh, PA
Dawn Gibbs	Principal	Pensacola, FL
Shannon H. Gibson	SPED Language Arts/Reading Teacher	Bowling Green, KY
Deb Giddey	Pre-K Teacher	Warren, MI
Bethany Gillespie	Elementary Special Education	Des Moines, IA
Lydia Goodwin	3rd Grade	Evansville, IN
Liz Grier	Teacher	Des Moines, IA
Shelby Grizzard	5th Grade Teacher	Richmond Hill, GA
Lindsay Gunier	SPED Teacher	Joliet, IL
Carolyn Gutowski	Fourth Grade Teacher	Liverpool, NY
Tammy Hall Westmark	School Counselor	Pensacola, FL
Jennifer Hammond	Teacher	Rochester, NY
Cheryl Handley	Special Ed Director	Douglasville, GA
Dr. Sarah Hartman	Department Chair	Henderson, TN
Sharonda Hector	Teacher of Deportment	Springfield, MA
Kim Heim	Special Education Teacher	Boone, IA
Stephen Hickson ED.D	Teacher/Coach	Brunswick, GA
Patricia Hiemer	ELA Teacher	Plainfield, IL

Katie R. Hildebrand	High School ESOL Teacher	Brunswick, GA
Melissa Hill	Social Studies Teacher	Joliet, IL
Michelle Honoway Sobkoviak	Principal	Milford, IL
Billy Hueramo	Principal	DeKalb, IL
Jamie Hughes	MS SPED Teacher	Covington, IN
Jessica M. Humphrey	Intervention Specialist	Cleveland, OH
Tonya L. Hunskor	K-12 Principal	Granville, ND
MaElena Ingram	Spanish I	McAllen, TX
Jeniifer Jacobs	ARC SCSEL	Brunswick, GA
Matthew Jenkins	Assistant Principal	Cedar Rapids, IA
Tracy Jimmerson	First Grade Teacher	Douglas, AL
Jen Johnson	Special Education Instructional Coach	Fond du Lac, WI
Lisa Johnson	High School Nurse	Buffalo, NY
Eric Johnson	8th Grade Teacher	Maryland Hts., MO
Jennifer Johnson	Instructional Coach	Council Bluffs, IA
Amy Johnson	5th Grade Teacher	Joliet, IL
Cheryll Jude	Cafeteria Manager	Galloway, OH
Dawn Jurgensen	CDA/Preschool Para	Cherokee, IA
Erin Kaiser	K-5 ELL Teacher	Des Moines, IA
Emily Keberlein	Special Education Teacher	Fort Dodge, IA
Wendy Kee	Guidance Counselor	Guntersville, AL
Denise Kelly	Kindergarten Teacher	Pulaski NY
Jessica Kennedy	Pre-K Teacher	Warren, MI
Patricia Kinser	Teacher	Mt. Healthy, OH
Carolyn Kintisch	Special Ed Teacher	Rochester, NY
Elisa Kirby	4th Grade Teacher	Cheektowaga, NY
Jill Klich	1st Grade Teacher	Ralston, NE
Raina Klisch	1st Grade Teacher	Springfield, MN
Jolene Koehler	School Psychologist	Bath, NY
Katie Kollmar	Teacher Aide	Tonawanda, NY
Sharon Krasner	ELA Teacher	Southfield, MI
Rachele Laminman	Kindergarten Teacher	Pahoa, HI
Tricia Langholdt-Vannatta	Preschool Teacher	Cherokee, IA
Lindsay Laske	Teacher	Raleigh, NC
Sara Lehman	Special Education Teacher	Des Moines, IA
Richard Lehr	Behavioral Intervention Specialist	Lackawanna, NY
Crystal Lembke	3rd Grade Teacher	Wanatah, IN
Sheila Levesque	Principal	Charlotte, NC
Stephanie Levy	4th Grade Teacher	Brunswick, GA
Melissa Leyen	Head Start Coordinator	Des Moines, IA
Katie Libbra	Special Education Teacher	Roxana, IL
Mary Little	Alternative Education	Verona, NY

Maria Lorant-Bronold	5th Grade Science Teacher	Mission, TX
Angie Lorenz	Instructional Coach	Urbandale, IA
Adrienne Mann	SPED Teacher	Cicero, IL
Mary Mantelli	Principal	Geneva, NY
Lori Maxeiner	Learning Support Teacher: K-3	Saegertown, PA
Katie McClain	1st Grade Teacher	Wanatah, IN
Amy McCloskey	Director of Pupil Services	Jamestown, NY
Lisa McDaniel Perkins	Paraprofessional	Dansville, NY
Laura McDonald	Educational Sales Consultant	Indian Trail, NC
Alicia Meyer	5th Grade ELA	Evansville, IN
Rachel Meyers	2nd Grade	Fairfield, IA
Dr. Steve Miletto	Executive Director	Dublin, GA
Kristen Miller	Special Education Teacher, DI Coach	Horseheads, NY
Leslie Miller	Alternative School Coordinator	Bowling Green, KY
Jennifer Mitchell	2nd Grade Teacher	Sumter, SC
Becky Mitchell Murphy	ELA 6th Grade Teacher	Pickerington, OH
Joanna Mock	Director	Mt. Vernon, GA
Jamie Monaco	High School Special Ed Teacher	Jamestown, NY
Rachel Montgomery	Assistant Principal	McAllen, TX
Katie Mooney	Teacher	Rochester, NY
Kelly Morken	Second Grade Teacher	Ames, IA
Lori Morris	Principal	Bowling Green, KY
Devon Morrison	4th Grade Teacher	Richmond Hill, GA
Angela Murray	7th Grade ELA Teacher	Bowling Green, KY
Ashley Nabors	5th Grade Teacher	Baltimore, MD
Yousef Nasouf	Principal	La Puente, CA
Kathleen Neefe	Teacher Assistant	Hilton, NY
Pam Nickelson	Special Education	League City, TX
Joey Norman	Assistant Principal	Bowling Green, KY
Virgina Nunez	1st Grade Teacher	Buckeye, AZ
Laura Odeen	K-5 Music Teacher	Des Moines, IA
Greg Opalinski	Mathematics Teacher	Lackawanna, NY
Whitney Ott-Zuzich	Middle School Teacher	Jesup, IA
Chrissy Owenby	Special Education Coordinator	Toccoa, GA
Nicole Palmer (Phillips)	Behavior Specialist	Buffalo, NY
Alison Patton	Special Education	Richmond Hill, GA
Alice Pewick	Special Education Teacher	Ames, IA
Mary Lou Pierret	5th Grade Teacher	Saegertown, PA
Erin Pilling	2nd Grade Teacher	Glasgow, KY
Anna M. Poole	3rd Grade Teacher	Saegertown, PA
Cynthia Porchas-Navarro	MS Teacher	Winterhaven, CA
Becky Priefer	Intervention Specialist	Akron, OH

Teresa Quibell (TQ)	Special Education Teacher	Rochester, NY
Kaitlin Rando	English Teacher	Harrisburg, PA
Sara Rather	3rd Grade Teacher	Bowling Green, KY
Nancy Redican	8th Grade Teacher	Palmdale, CA
Teresa Reed	Assistant Principal	Pembroke, GA
Erica Reichard	2nd Grade Teacher	Sherburne, NY
Denise Reinert	Instructional Coach	Indianola, IN
Diana Riemenschneider	Teacher	Mt. Healthy, OH
Cat Rinella	SPED Teacher	Sidney, NY
Nicole Rodgers	4-6th Counselor	Pekin, IL
Amy Rodriguez	Resource Teacher	Palm Bay, FL
Brooke Rosenau	NDCPD Infant Development	Minot, ND
Carla Roth	Kindergarten Teacher	Omaha, NE
Crystal Rouse	Special Education Teacher	Montgomery County, MD
Jilliane Runigham	Alternative Education Youth Worker	PEI, Canada
Shelia Santangelo Madore	Middle School Teacher	Akron, NY
Sylvia Sattler	Educator	Mojave, CA
Gretchen Schaefer	Director of Academic Achievement	Peru, IL
Kirsten Schober	6th Grade ELA	Newnan, GA
Angela Scholl	Middle School Dean of Students	Maquoketa, IA
Julia Schroeder	Dean of Students	Charlotte, NC
Derek Schultz	Special Education Teacher	Des Moines, IA
Kristy Schumacher	2nd Grade Teacher	Minneota, MN
Dana Schuster	Special Ed Teacher	Minooka, IL
Allie Segarra	2nd Grade Teacher	St. John, ND
Reba Serrano	Music Teacher	Whiteriver, AZ
Terryl Shimizu	2nd Grade Teacher	Bowling Green, KY
Marie Shipley	2nd Grade Teacher	Ames, IA
Tracy Short	Special Education Teacher	Rochester, NY
Jennifer Silverman	ELA Teacher	Plainfield, IL
Michelle Simons	Focus Program	Des Moines, IA
Erin Sirmon	Kindergarten Teacher	Luling, LA
Holly Sitzmann	Special Education Teacher	Jesup, IA
Lori Skelton	Principal	Rochester, NY
Jessica Skoryi	3rd Grade Teacher	Crest Hill, IL
Elizabeth Skwarczynski	Social Studies	Joliet, IL
Laurie Slaughter	1st Grade Teacher	Richmond Hill, GA
Karen Smith	Elementary Principal	Richmond Hill, GA
Emily-Kaye Smith	6th Grade Teacher	Bowling Green, KY
Olivia Smith	Speech Language Pathologist	Nashville, TN
Cindy Snow	3rd Grade Teacher	Warrensburg, MO
Tia Sommerville	8th Grade Language Arts	Bowling Green, KY

Shelly Starline	7th Grade Reading Teacher	Cincinnati, OH
Lia Staszak	Special Education Teacher	Rochester, NY
Melissa Statman	Science Teacher	Meadville, PA
Jennifer Stechmann	SPED Teacher	Mobile, AL
Brittany Stewart	English Teacher	Bowling Green, KY
Sherry Strough	SPED Teacher	Indianapolis, IN
Matt Struzik	7-12 ELA	Attica, NY
Rebecca Studer	4th Grade Teacher	Des Moines, IA
Nicole Stuhldryer	Special Education Teacher	Des Moines, IA
Jessica Suva	ELA	Joliet, IL
Jodi Swett	BD Teacher	Des Moines, IA
Danielle Taylor	Instructional Coach	Des Moines, IA
Kim Thayer	School Administrative Manager	Carter Lake, IA
Lisa Thielen	EBD Teacher	Fairmont, MN
Chrissy Thoele	7th Grade ELA	Plainfield, IL
Sunshine Thomas-Bear	Special Education Teacher	Winnebago, NE
Suzanna Tobe	Teacher	Mt. Healthy, OH
Dixie Todaro	2nd Grade Teacher	Luling, LA
Holly Touranjoe	2nd Grade Teacher	Syracuse, NY
Louisa Tsuchida	Intervention Specialist	Dayton, OH
Aly Tuttle	K-2 Special Ed Teacher	Grinnell, IA
Trisha Tynan	Second Grade Teacher	Pulaski, NY
Natalie Urbas	Intervention Specialist	Painesville Twp., OH
Merlyna Valentine	Retired Principal/National Speaker	LaPlace, LA
Jane Van Alstyne	6-8 Resource Inclusivion	Palmdale, CA
Sherie Van Berkum	Behavior Interventionist	Alta, IA
Kim Van Gundy	Special Education Teacher	Des Moines, IA
Jenni Van Otterloo	Special Education Teacher	Sanborn, IA
Becky Vanderhyden	Special Education Teacher	Joliet, IL
Rosa Vazquez	SEL Teacher	Indianapolis, IN
Veronica Velazquez	Special Education Paraprofessional	Springfield, MA
Ashley Vincent	Librarian	Bowling Green, KY
Andrew Wade	Dean of Students	Des Moines, IA
John Walje IV	Teacher	Wahiawa, HI
Michelle Walker	First Grade Teacher	Douglas, AL
Amber Warner	Biology Teacher	Greenville, OH
Kim Waters	Read 180 Teacher Grades 3-5	Brunswick, GA
Audra Watson	Behavior Coach	Ames, IA
Stefanie Wells	Head Start Teacher	Des Moines, IA
Nathan West	Special Education Teacher	Westville, IL
Rosemary West	Title One	Lawrenceville, IL
Kate Westphal	6th Grade Math & Social Studies	Aurelia, IA

Annette Wiederholt	High School Math Teacher	Rosemead, CA
Sarah Wiggins	Principal	Binghamton, NY
Amanda Williams	1st Grade Teacher	Bowling Green, KY
Kaci Wilson	Secondary ELA Teacher	Bowling Green, NY
Eric Wilson	Principal	Bowling Green, KY
Dawn Winkelmann	Niagara Preschool Learning Center	Sanborn, NY
Melanie Wyatt	Alternative Teacher	Bowling Green, KY
Amy Yates	5th Grade Teacher	Alvaton, KY